ELEVENTH EDITION

THE

BLUE BOOK

OF GRAMMAR AND PUNCTUATION

An Easy-to-Use Guide with Clear Rules,
Real-World Examples, and Reproducible Quizzes

Jane Straus

Lester Kaufman

Edited with new material by Tom Stern

JOSSEY-BASS™

A Wiley Brand

Copyright ©2014 by Lester Kaufman. All rights reserved.
Published by Jossey-Bass
A Wiley Brand
One Montgomery Street, Suite 1200, San Francisco, CA 94104-4594—www.josseybass.com

Jossey-Bass books and products are available through most bookstores. To contact Jossey-Bass directly call our Customer Care Department within the U.S. at 800-956-7739, outside the U.S. at 317-572-3986, or fax 317-572-4002.

Wiley publishes in a variety of print and electronic formats and by print-on-demand. Some material included with standard print versions of this book may not be included in e-books or in print-on-demand. If this book refers to media such as a CD or DVD that is not included in the version you purchased, you may download this material at http://booksupport.wiley.com. For more information about Wiley products, visit www.wiley.com.

Library of Congress Cataloging-in-Publication Data

Straus, Jane.
 The blue book of grammar and punctuation : an easy-to-use guide with clear rules, real-world examples, and reproducible quizzes / Jane Straus, Lester Kaufman, Tom Stern.—Eleventh edition.
     pages cm
 Includes index.
     ISBN 978-1-118-78556-0 (pbk)—ISBN 978-1-118-79021-2 (pdf)—ISBN 978-1-118-79032-8 (epub)
 1. English language—Grammar. 2. English language—Grammar—Problems, exercises, etc. 3. English language—Punctuation. 4. English language—Punctuation—Problems, exercises, etc. I. Kaufman, Lester II. Stern, Tom III. Title.
 PE1112.S773 2014
 428.2—dc23

2013038993

Printed in the United States of America

ELEVENTH EDITION

PB Printing 10 9 8 7 6 5 4 3 2 1

CONTENTS

Preface and Acknowledgments   xv

About the Authors   xvii

Introduction   xix

1 GRAMMAR   1

Finding Nouns, Verbs, and Subjects   1

    Definitions

        Noun

        Verb

        Subject

    Using verbs to find subjects

    Multiple subjects and verbs in a sentence

    Infinitives

    You as an understood subject

Subject-Verb Agreement   3

    Singular vs. plural verbs

    Finding subjects before phrases beginning with *of*

    With *or, either/or,* and *neither/nor*

        Two singular subjects

        One singular and one plural subject

With *and*
With interrupting expressions
With such portions as *percent, fraction, part,* etc.
With *here* or *there*
With distances, periods of time, sums of money, etc.
With collective nouns
The subjunctive mood

Clauses and Phrases 7

Definitions
    Clause
    Independent clause
    Dependent clause
    Phrase

Pronouns 7

Definition: Pronoun
Subject pronouns
    As the subject of the sentence
    Renaming the subject
    When *who* refers to a personal pronoun
Object pronouns
Subject and verb agreement with *who, that,* and *which*
Subject and verb agreement with *anyone, someone, each,* etc.
Following *than* or *as*
Possessive pronouns
Its vs. *it's; who's* vs. *whose*
Reflexives: the *-self* pronouns
Consistency with singular pronouns
Pronouns linked with nouns by *and*

Who vs. Whom 12

He/him method
Common *whom* pitfall

Whoever vs. Whomever 13

Agreement with the verb in the dependent clause
Dependent clause as the subject of the verb following the clause

Who, That, Which 14

Who, that, and *which* with people, groups, and things
That with essential clauses
Which with nonessential clauses
When *which* can be used with essential clauses

Adjectives and Adverbs 15

Definitions
    Adjective
    Adverb
Adjectives modifying nouns and pronouns
Adverbs modifying verbs, adjectives, and adverbs
When to add *-ly*
Sense verbs: *taste, smell, look, feel,* etc.
Good vs. *well*
Well as an adjective when referring to health
Comparisons, such as *-er* vs. *-est* and *more* vs. *most*
This, that, these, and *those*

Prepositions 18

Definition: preposition
Ending a sentence with a preposition
    Avoiding extra prepositions
Like
As, as if, as though, the way
Of vs. *have*
Different from vs. *different than*
In vs. *into*

Effective Writing 20

Concrete vs. vague language
Active vs. passive voice
Overuse of *there is, there are, it is, it was,* etc.
Double negatives
Parallel construction
Dangling modifiers
Misplaced modifiers
Fragments

2 PUNCTUATION   25

Periods   25

    With complete sentences
    With abbreviations at the end of a sentence
    Replacing periods with question marks and exclamation points

Commas   25

    To separate three or more items
    To separate adjectives
    With two independent clauses
        Run-on sentences or comma splices
        Joined by connectors such as *and, or, but,* etc.
        When the subject does not appear in front of the second verb
    With introductory words
    To set off interrupting expressions
    With names
    With dates
    With city and state
    With *Jr.* and *Sr.*
    With degrees and titles
    Starting a sentence with a dependent clause vs. an independent clause
    With nonessential words, clauses, and phrases
    With sufficiently identified noun
    With quotations
        To introduce or interrupt quotations
        Following quotations
    To separate statements from questions
    To separate contrasting parts of a sentence
    With certain introductory words
        When followed by a series of items
        When the series of items ends with *etc.*

Semicolons   30

    To replace a period in two closely linked sentences
    With such words as *namely, however, therefore,* etc., when they
    introduce a complete sentence
    To avoid confusion where commas already exist
    With sentences that have multiple clauses

Colons   **31**

To introduce a series of items
Except when a series of items directly follows a verb or preposition
With lists
With two independent clauses when the second explains the first
With long quotations
After the salutation in a business letter

Quotation Marks   **33**

Use of double quotation marks
With titles of magazines, books, plays, etc.
With periods and commas
 ALWAYS inside quotation marks
 Use of single quotation marks for quotations within quotations
Spacing between single and double quotation marks
With nonstandard expressions
 With technical terms and terms used in an unusual way
 Avoiding single quotation marks
With quoted material of more than one paragraph

Parentheses and Brackets   **34**

Not interchangeable
Parentheses   34
 For clarification and asides
 With complete sentences
 Subject-verb agreement
 Comma placement with parentheses
Brackets   35
 With interruptions
 Use of [*sic*]
 With quotations

Apostrophes   **36**

Singular nouns
 Possession with singular nouns
 Possession with common nouns ending in *s*
 Possession with proper nouns ending in *s*
Plural nouns
 Plural possession with regular nouns
 No apostrophe with regular nouns

Plural possession with irregular nouns
Plural possession with names ending in *s*
No apostrophe with plural names
Possession with singular compound nouns
To show joint possession
Contractions
With initials, capital letters, and numbers used as nouns
With time or money
With personal pronouns
Apostrophes vs. single quotation marks
False possessives
With nouns ending in *y*

Hyphens   40

Hyphens between words   41
With compound adjectives
With compound verbs
With compound nouns
With *very* and *-ly* adverbs
With ages
For clarification
With spans of time, distance, or other quantities
With compound numbers
With spelled-out fractions
With double last names
Avoiding overuse
Look it up
Hyphens with prefixes and suffixes   43
Prefixes with proper nouns or proper adjectives
Prefixes with double vowels
With *self-*, *ex-*, and *all-*
With *re-*
To avoid confusion
Suffixes not usually hyphenated
Suffixes and double letters
Using discretion and a dictionary

Dashes   45

Dashes and subject agreement
In place of other punctuation
Spacing

Ellipses 46

    Definition and three-dot method
    With omitted words or sentences
    To express hesitation, changes of mood, etc.

Question Marks 47

    With direct questions
    Replacing periods
        Capitalization following a question mark
    Indirect questions
        Rhetorical questions
    With sentences that are half statement and half question
    With quotation marks

Exclamation Points 48

    To show emotion, emphasis, or surprise
    Replacing periods
    Avoidance in formal business writing
    Justifiable use

3   CAPITALIZATION 49

    First word of a document and after a period
    Proper nouns and adjectives derived from proper nouns
        Reference list of capitalized categories
        Reference list of lowercase categories
    Thorny aspects of capitalization
    Titles
    Titles vs. occupations
    Titles in direct address
        Kinship names
        Nicknames
    Geographic regions vs. points of the compass
    The before proper nouns
    City, town, county, etc., before a proper name
    First word of a quotation
    Midsentence independent clauses or questions
    Course titles vs. academic subjects
    Art movements
    Lists following colons

Lowercase *the national anthem*
Titles of books, plays, films, songs, etc.
    Subtitles

4   WRITING NUMBERS   57

Using figures vs. spelling out numbers
Numbers beginning a sentence
Hyphenating compound numbers
    Hyphenating fractions
Figures of four or more digits
    Sums less than a dollar
Noon and midnight
    Time of day
Mixed fractions
Large numbers
Decimals
When to use *and*
Dates
Decades
    Use lowercase when spelling out
    Using apostrophes with incomplete numerals
    Avoiding apostrophe + *s* with complete numerals

5   CONFUSING WORDS AND HOMONYMS   61

Imply vs. infer
Lay vs. lie
Their vs. there vs. they're
Hundreds more words and homonyms that perplex and confound

6   QUIZZES   125

Grammar *Pretest*   125

Finding Nouns, Verbs, and Subjects *Quiz 1*   127

Finding Nouns, Verbs, and Subjects *Quiz 2*   127

Subject and Verb Agreement *Quiz 1*   **128**

Subject and Verb Agreement *Quiz 2*   **129**

Pronouns *Quiz 1*   **130**

Pronouns *Quiz 2*   **131**

Who, Whom, Whoever, Whomever *Quiz 1*   **131**

Who, Whom, Whoever, Whomever *Quiz 2*   **132**

Who, Whom, That, Which *Quiz 1*   **133**

Who, Whom, That, Which *Quiz 2*   **134**

Adjectives and Adverbs *Quiz 1*   **134**

Adjectives and Adverbs *Quiz 2*   **135**

Prepositions *Quiz 1*   **136**

Prepositions *Quiz 2*   **136**

Affect vs. Effect *Quiz 1*   **137**

Affect vs. Effect *Quiz 2*   **137**

Lay vs. Lie *Quiz 1*   **138**

Lay vs. Lie *Quiz 2*   **139**

Advice vs. Advise *Quiz 1*   **139**

Advice vs. Advise *Quiz 2*   **140**

Their vs. There vs. They're *Quiz 1*   **140**

Their vs. There vs. They're *Quiz 2*   **141**

More Confusing Words and Homonyms *Quiz 1*   **141**

More Confusing Words and Homonyms *Quiz 2*   **142**

Effective Writing *Quiz 1*   **142**

Effective Writing *Quiz 2*   **143**

Grammar Mastery *Test*   **144**

Punctuation, Capitalization, and Writing Numbers *Pretest*   **145**

Commas and Periods *Quiz 1*   **147**

Commas and Periods *Quiz 2*   **148**

Semicolons and Colons *Quiz 1*   149

Semicolons and Colons *Quiz 2*   150

Question Marks and Quotation Marks *Quiz 1*   151

Question Marks and Quotation Marks *Quiz 2*   152

Parentheses and Brackets *Quiz 1*   152

Parentheses and Brackets *Quiz 2*   153

Apostrophes *Quiz 1*   153

Apostrophes *Quiz 2*   154

Hyphens Between Words *Quiz 1*   154

Hyphens Between Words *Quiz 2*   155

Hyphens with Prefixes and Suffixes *Quiz 1*   156

Hyphens with Prefixes and Suffixes *Quiz 2*   156

Capitalization *Quiz 1*   157

Capitalization *Quiz 2*   157

Writing Numbers *Quiz 1*   158

Writing Numbers *Quiz 2*   158

Punctuation, Capitalization, and Writing Numbers Mastery *Test*   159

7 ANSWERS TO QUIZZES 161

Grammar *Pretest Answers*   161

Finding Nouns, Verbs, and Subjects *Quiz 1 Answers*   163

Finding Nouns, Verbs, and Subjects *Quiz 2 Answers*   163

Subject and Verb Agreement *Quiz 1 Answers*   164

Subject and Verb Agreement *Quiz 2 Answers*   165

Pronouns *Quiz 1 Answers*   165

Pronouns *Quiz 2 Answers*   166

Who, Whom, Whoever, Whomever *Quiz 1 Answers* 167

Who, Whom, Whoever, Whomever *Quiz 2 Answers* 168

Who, Whom, That, Which *Quiz 1 Answers* 168

Who, Whom, That, Which *Quiz 2 Answers* 169

Adjectives and Adverbs *Quiz 1 Answers* 169

Adjectives and Adverbs *Quiz 2 Answers* 170

Prepositions *Quiz 1 Answers* 171

Prepositions *Quiz 2 Answers* 171

Affect vs. Effect *Quiz 1 Answers* 172

Affect vs. Effect *Quiz 2 Answers* 172

Lay vs. Lie *Quiz 1 Answers* 173

Lay vs. Lie *Quiz 2 Answers* 173

Advice vs. Advise *Quiz 1 Answers* 174

Advice vs. Advise *Quiz 2 Answers* 174

Their vs. There vs. They're *Quiz 1 Answers* 175

Their vs. There vs. They're *Quiz 2 Answers* 175

More Confusing Words and Homonyms *Quiz 1 Answers* 176

More Confusing Words and Homonyms *Quiz 2 Answers* 176

Effective Writing *Quiz 1 Answers* 177

Effective Writing *Quiz 2 Answers* 178

Grammar Mastery *Test Answers* 179

Punctuation, Capitalization, and Writing Numbers *Pretest Answers* 181

Commas and Periods *Quiz 1 Answers* 182

Commas and Periods *Quiz 2 Answers* 183

Semicolons and Colons *Quiz 1 Answers* 184

Semicolons and Colons *Quiz 2 Answers* 185

Question Marks and Quotation Marks *Quiz 1 Answers*   **186**

Question Marks and Quotation Marks *Quiz 2 Answers*   **186**

Parentheses and Brackets *Quiz 1 Answers*   **187**

Parentheses and Brackets *Quiz 2 Answers*   **187**

Apostrophes *Quiz 1 Answers*   **188**

Apostrophes *Quiz 2 Answers*   **188**

Hyphens Between Words *Quiz 1 Answers*   **189**

Hyphens Between Words *Quiz 2 Answers*   **189**

Hyphens with Prefixes and Suffixes *Quiz 1 Answers*   **190**

Hyphens with Prefixes and Suffixes *Quiz 2 Answers*   **190**

Capitalization *Quiz 1 Answers*   **191**

Capitalization *Quiz 2 Answers*   **191**

Writing Numbers *Quiz 1 Answers*   **192**

Writing Numbers *Quiz 2 Answers*   **192**

Punctuation, Capitalization, and Writing Numbers Mastery *Test Answers*   **193**

Index   **195**

PREFACE AND ACKNOWLEDGMENTS

Jane Straus created her English language instructional materials because she "found no books that conveyed the rules of English in—well—plain English." Over the years of teaching basic English language skills to state and federal government employees as well as to individuals in the private sector and in nonprofit organizations, she refined her materials, eventually creating *The Blue Book of Grammar and Punctuation* and its related website, GrammarBook.com.

In the introduction to the tenth edition, the author spoke of her 2003 brain tumor diagnosis, how it led to her next bold steps in life, and her successful surgery to remove the tumor. Unfortunately, in 2009, she again learned she had a new, unrelated brain tumor—this time malignant. Jane Ruth Straus passed away on February 25, 2011.

Due to the outpouring of appreciation for her work, her husband, Lester Kaufman, continued to oversee the GrammarBook.com website so that anyone around the world could still benefit from her life's work. He also collected ideas and suggestions for changes, new material, and improvements to *The Blue Book*. After making the acquaintance of Tom Stern, a Marin County, California, writer and editor, Kaufman recognized that Stern possessed the knowledge, skills, experience, and passion needed to thoroughly re-examine *The Blue Book* and revise it to make it a first-rate grammar resource for everyone.

First and foremost, thanks must go to the late Jane Straus for her vision and persistence in creating a reference guide and workbook that is popular and easy to understand. We could not have succeeded in updating this book without the assistance of Marjorie McAneny at Jossey-Bass and literary agent Cathy Fowler, both of whom steadfastly believed in the book's value. We also thank Zoe Kaufman, Jojo Ortiz, and Patti Clements, for their contributions to the quizzes; the thousands of loyal readers and viewers of the GrammarBook.com website who, by offering valuable input daily, have helped shape the rules, examples, and quizzes; and Gary Klehr, for helping name the book many years ago.

This book is dedicated to my brilliant wife, Jane Straus. She was a multitalented woman with boundless energy and a natural gift for clarifying all matters complex. She put her heart and soul into everything she undertook. She was taken from us far too soon.

—LESTER KAUFMAN

ABOUT THE AUTHORS

JANE STRAUS (1954–2011) was an educator, life coach, and best-selling author. To prepare for a job teaching English to employees of the state of California in 1975, Straus scoured the library for materials that conveyed the rules of English in plain English. Finding no such resources, she wrote the rules her own way, made up exercises, ran off some copies, and hoped for the best.

The class was a hit. More and more state employees demanded that they get an equal opportunity to benefit from Straus's no-nonsense instruction in English grammar and usage. She continued to refine her materials, eventually turning them into *The Blue Book of Grammar and Punctuation*.

When the Internet was born, she launched a website, GrammarBook.com, which has helped millions of people all over the world improve their English grammar. Straus became a sought-after speaker in the fields of grammar, public speaking, and life coaching. Her other book is *Enough Is Enough! Stop Enduring and Start Living Your Extraordinary Life* (Jossey-Bass, 2005).

LESTER KAUFMAN is the publisher of GrammarBook.com. A lifelong public servant, he served first in the Peace Corps, and eventually completed the final years of his federal career with the U.S. Environmental Protection Agency. He married Jane Straus in 1987.

After his retirement from the EPA, Kaufman began assisting with the operation of Straus's fledgling website and helped edit previous editions of *The Blue Book of Grammar and Punctuation*.

Following Jane Straus's untimely passing in early 2011, Kaufman assumed management of GrammarBook.com, which features an informative and entertaining weekly newsletter that encourages readers to ask grammar questions and offer their views on the state of twenty-first-century English.

TOM STERN is a freelance writer and editor. After leaving a career in the music business in 1992, he became a copyeditor-reporter-critic, eventually working for a number of San Francisco Bay Area periodicals. In 2011, his twice-monthly grammar column for a Marin County newspaper chain placed first in the California Newspaper Publishers Association's Better Newspapers Contest.

INTRODUCTION

Now in its eleventh edition, *The Blue Book of Grammar and Punctuation* will help you write and speak with confidence. You don't have to be an English major to understand grammar and punctuation. You just need rules and guidelines that are easy to understand, with real-world examples.

Whether you are an instructor teaching students the rules of English or a student, executive, professional writer, or avid blogger honing your grammar and punctuation skills, this book will help you zip through tests (including the SAT), reports, essays, letters, e-mails, and résumés. It will help you (and your writing) impress your teachers, your clients, and other readers.

Every generation of English scholars despairs because the language always seems to be at a crisis point. But it is undeniable that everywhere one looks nowadays, the principles in this book are casually and cavalierly violated.

The Blue Book will prove to be a valuable tool for teachers and students in achieving the goals of the Common Core State Standards Initiative. Studying the chapters and working through the quizzes will provide students of all ages with the skills and knowledge they need to succeed beyond high school—in college and in the workplace. Students will learn how to use formal English in their writing and speaking and how to better express themselves through language. We also recommend reading the works of great writers to experience firsthand the art and beauty of effective communication.

This book is logical, self-paced, and fun to use, with scores of interesting and challenging quizzes that you may photocopy to your heart's content. Best of all, you can look forward to instant gratification, because the answers to the quizzes are included.

Throughout the text, certain terms have been set in boldface type (for instance, at the beginning of Chapter One, **noun, common nouns, proper nouns**). Due to space and other considerations, we could not always explore these linguistic terms as thoroughly as we might have wished. Readers are strongly urged to look further into these terms on their own. We also recommend that those who are serious about improving their English grammar always keep a dictionary close by and use it assiduously.

If you don't have time to research several leading reference books to figure out where the next comma should go or whether to write *who* or *whom*, you will find *The Blue Book* to be a pleasure to use. Dedicated to eliminating unnecessary jargon, it highlights the most important grammar, punctuation, and capitalization rules and guidelines and clarifies some of the language's most confusing and confounding words.

In Chapter One, "Grammar," you will learn how to find nouns, verbs, and subjects and make sure they agree with one another. Next you will learn about clauses and phrases, the keys to understanding sentence structure. Then, on to pronoun usage, so that you will know whether to write *I* or *me, he* or *him, who* or *whom*, etc. From there, in the "Adjectives and Adverbs" section, you will discover why some words have *-ly* added to them, and why you must say, "She did well on the test," rather than "She did good on the test." After that, you will breeze through prepositions, learning some surprising rules, and we will debunk at least one myth. (*Hint*: Is it safe to ask, "What are you talking about?" or must we ask, "About what are you talking?")

The "Effective Writing" section of Chapter One will give you helpful tips for constructing sentences and paragraphs that flow gracefully, making it easier to write quickly and well.

Chapter Two, "Punctuation," takes on all the usual suspects: periods, commas, semicolons, colons, quotation marks, parentheses and brackets, apostrophes, hyphens, dashes, ellipses, question marks, and exclamation points. The best part about this and other chapters is that you will find an abundance of examples that you run across every day.

Then comes Chapter Three, "Capitalization," in which you will get your most vexing questions answered, learning which words to capitalize in a title and when to capitalize job titles, such as *president* or *director*.

In Chapter Four, "Writing Numbers," you will learn the importance of consistency when using numerals or writing out numbers. You will also learn how to write fractions and large numbers.

After that, you will enjoy spending time reading all about *affect* vs. *effect, lay* vs. *lie, their* vs. *there* vs. *they're*, and *its* vs. *it's* in Chapter Five, "Confusing Words and Homonyms." We have provided hundreds of words and phrases for you in this chapter, so you will never again have to be confused by the differences between *farther* and *further, continual* and *continuous, flaunt* and *flout, tortuous* and *torturous*, and all the rest of the trickiest and most commonly misused words and phrases in the English language.

Promise not to skip the quizzes, pretests, or mastery tests in Chapter Six. The more you practice, the more confident you will become. Once you get over any fears about test taking, we think you will find the quizzes both enjoyable and challenging. You will find the answers in Chapter Seven.

Please visit www.GrammarBook.com, where you will find all the quizzes in the book in a multiple-choice, interactive format. If you are a teacher or are really jazzed about improving your English skills, on the website you will also find

- Hundreds of additional downloadable, interactive quizzes in the "Subscription" area
- Dozens of free one-minute videos by Jane Straus on English language usage
- All the rules and examples you see in the book
- A sign-up box on the home page for our free weekly e-newsletter with tips and articles
- Our blog
- Recommendations for further reading and study

The point of grammar proficiency is to be clear and direct, and to avoid misunderstanding. We hope you will come away from this book with this mantra: "Think before you write." Be sure every sentence conveys what you mean, with no possibility of ambiguity or inadvertent meaninglessness.

That being said, as George Orwell wrote in 1946, "Break any of these rules sooner than say anything outright barbarous."

We hope you find *The Blue Book* to be both enjoyable and invaluable.

The authors researched the leading reference books on American English grammar and punctuation including *The Chicago Manual of Style, The Associated Press Stylebook*, Fowler's *Modern English Usage*, Bernstein's *The Careful Writer*, and many others. The authors provide rules, guidance, and examples based on areas of general agreement among the authorities. Where the authorities differ, this book provides options to follow based on the reader's purpose in writing, with this general advice: be consistent.

CHAPTER 1

GRAMMAR

FINDING NOUNS, VERBS, AND SUBJECTS

> **NOTE**
> We will use the standard of underlining subjects once and verbs twice.

Definitions

- A **noun** is a word or set of words for a person, place, thing, or idea. A noun of more than one word (*tennis court, gas station*) is called a **compound noun**.

There are **common nouns** and **proper nouns**. Common nouns are words for a general class of people, places, things, and ideas (*man, city, award, honesty*). They are not capitalized. Proper nouns are always capitalized. They name specific people, places, and things (*Joe, Chicago, Academy Award*).

For more on nouns, see Chapter Two, "Apostrophes," Rules 2a through 2e.

- A **verb** is a word or set of words that shows action (*runs, is going, has been painting*); feeling (*loves, envies*); or state of being (*am, are, is, have been, was, seem*).

Examples: He <u>ran</u> around the block.
                    I <u>like</u> my friend.
                    They <u>seem</u> friendly.

State-of-being verbs are called **linking verbs**. They include all forms of the verb *to be*, plus such words as *look, feel, appear, act, go*, followed by an adjective. (See the "Adjectives and Adverbs" section later in this chapter.)

Examples: You *look* happy.
                    We *feel fine.*
                    He *went* ballistic.

Verbs often consist of more than one word. For instance, *had been breaking down* is a four-word verb. It has a two-word main verb, *breaking down* (also called a **phrasal verb**), and two **helping verbs** (*had* and *been*). Helping verbs are so named because they help clarify the intended meaning.

Many verbs can function as helping verbs, including *is, shall, must, do, has, can, keep, get, start, help*, etc.

- A **subject** is the noun, pronoun (see the "Pronouns" section later in this chapter), or set of words that performs the verb.

Examples: The woman hurried.
                    Woman is the subject.
                    She was late.
                    She is the subject.
                    Shakespeare in Love *won an Academy Award.*
                    Shakespeare in Love is the subject.

Rule 1. To find the subject and verb, always find the verb first. Then ask who or what performed the verb.

Examples: The jet engine **passed** inspection.
                    Passed is the verb. Who or what passed? The engine, so *engine* is the subject. (If you included the word *jet* as the subject, lightning will not strike you. But technically, *jet* is an adjective here and is part of what is known as the complete subject.)
                    From the ceiling **hung** the chandelier.
                    The verb is *hung*. Now, if you think *ceiling* is the subject, slow down. Ask *who* or *what* hung. The answer is the chandelier, not the ceiling. Therefore, *chandelier* is the subject.

Rule 2. Sentences can have more than one subject and more than one verb.

> *Examples*:   *I like cake, and he likes ice cream.* (Two subjects and two verbs)
> *He and I like cake.* (Two subjects and one verb)
> *She lifts weights and jogs daily.* (One subject and two verbs)

Rule 3. If a verb follows *to*, it is called an **infinitive**, and it is not the main verb. You will find the main verb either before or after the infinitive.

> *Examples*:   *He is trying to leave.*
> *To leave* is an infinitive; the main verb is *trying*.
> *To leave was his wish.*
> The main verb is *was*.

NOTE

One of the most stubborn superstitions in English is that it is wrong to insert a word between the *to* and the verb in an infinitive. This is called a **split infinitive** (*to **gladly** pay, to **not** go*). There is no English scholar alive who will say a split infinitive is technically wrong. However, split infinitives tend to be clumsy and unnecessary. Experienced writers do not use them without good reason.

Rule 4. Any request or command, such as *Stop!* or *Walk quickly*, has the understood subject *you*, because if we ask who is to stop or walk quickly, the answer must be "you."

> *Example*:   *(You) Please bring me some coffee.*
> *Bring* is the verb. Who will do the bringing? The subject *you* is understood.

SUBJECT-VERB AGREEMENT

Being able to find the right subject and verb will help you correct errors of subject-verb agreement.

Basic rule. A singular subject (*she, Bill, car*) takes a singular verb (*is, goes, shines*), whereas a plural subject takes a plural verb.

> *Example*:   *The list of items is/are on the desk.*
> If you know that *list* is the subject, then you will choose *is* for the verb.

Rule 1. A subject will come before a phrase beginning with *of*. This is a key rule for understanding subjects. The word *of* is the culprit in many, perhaps most, subject-verb mistakes.

Hasty writers, speakers, readers, and listeners might miss the all-too-common mistake in the following sentence:

> *Incorrect*:   *A bouquet of yellow roses lend color and fragrance to the room.*
> *Correct*:   *A <u>bouquet</u> of yellow roses <u>lends</u>. . . (bouquet lends, not roses lend)*

Rule 2. Two singular subjects connected by *or, either/or,* or *neither/nor* require a singular verb.

> *Examples*:   *My <u>aunt</u> or my <u>uncle</u> <u>is arriving</u> by train today.*
> *Neither <u>Juan</u> nor <u>Carmen</u> <u>is</u> available.*
> *Either <u>Kiana</u> or <u>Casey</u> <u>is</u> <u>helping</u> today with stage decorations.*

Rule 3. The verb in an *or, either/or,* or *neither/nor* sentence agrees with the noun or pronoun closest to it.

> *Examples*:   *Neither the <u>plates</u> nor the serving <u>bowl</u> <u>goes</u> on that shelf.*
> *Neither the serving <u>bowl</u> nor the <u>plates</u> <u>go</u> on that shelf.*

This rule can lead to bumps in the road. For example, if *I* is one of two (or more) subjects, it could lead to this odd sentence:

> *Awkward*:   *Neither she, my friends, nor I am going to the festival.*

If possible, it's best to reword such grammatically correct but awkward sentences.

> *Better*:   *Neither she, I, nor my friends are going to the festival.*
>   **OR**
>   *She, my friends, and I are not going to the festival.*

Rule 4. As a general rule, use a plural verb with two or more subjects when they are connected by *and*.

> *Example*:   *A <u>car</u> and a <u>bike</u> <u>are</u> my means of transportation.*

But note these exceptions:

> *Exceptions*:   *<u>Breaking and entering</u> <u>is</u> against the law.*
> *The <u>bed and breakfast</u> <u>was</u> charming.*

In those sentences, *breaking and entering* and *bed and breakfast* are compound nouns.

Rule 5. Sometimes the subject is separated from the verb by such words as *along with, as well as, besides, not,* etc. These words and phrases are not part of the subject. Ignore them and use a singular verb when the subject is singular.

Examples: The <u>politician</u>, along with the newsmen, <u>is expected</u> shortly.

<u>Excitement</u>, as well as nervousness, <u>is</u> the cause of her shaking.

Rule 6. With words that indicate portions—*percent, fraction, majority, some, all*, etc.—Rule 1 given earlier is reversed, and we are guided by the noun after *of*. If the noun after *of* is singular, use a singular verb. If it is plural, use a plural verb.

Examples: <u>Fifty percent</u> of the **pie** <u>has disappeared</u>.

<u>Fifty percent</u> of the **pies** <u>have disappeared</u>.

A <u>third</u> of the **city** <u>is</u> unemployed.

A <u>third</u> of the **people** <u>are</u> unemployed.

<u>All</u> of the **pie** <u>is</u> gone.

<u>All</u> of the **pies** <u>are</u> gone.

<u>Some</u> of the **pie** <u>is</u> missing.

<u>Some</u> of the **pies** <u>are</u> missing.

NOTE

In recent years, the SAT testing service has considered *none* to be strictly singular. However, according to *Merriam-Webster's Dictionary of English Usage*: "Clearly *none* has been both singular and plural since Old English and still is. The notion that it is singular only is a myth of unknown origin that appears to have arisen in the 19th century. If in context it seems like a singular to you, use a singular verb; if it seems like a plural, use a plural verb. Both are acceptable beyond serious criticism." When *none* is clearly intended to mean "not one," it is followed by a singular verb.

Rule 7. In sentences beginning with *here* or *there*, the true subject follows the verb.

Examples: There <u>are</u> four <u>hurdles</u> to jump.

There <u>is</u> a high <u>hurdle</u> to jump.

Here <u>are</u> the <u>keys</u>.

NOTE

The word *there's*, a contraction of *there is*, leads to bad habits in informal sentences like *There's a lot of people here today*, because it's easier to say "there's" than "there are." Take care never to use *there's* with a plural subject.

Rule 8. Use a singular verb with distances, periods of time, sums of money, etc., when considered as a unit.

> *Examples*: *Three miles **is** too far to walk.*
>
> *Five years **is** the maximum sentence for that offense.*
>
> *Ten dollars **is** a high price to pay.*
>
> **BUT**
>
> *Ten dollars (i.e., dollar bills) **were** scattered on the floor.*

Rule 9. Some collective nouns, such as *family, couple, staff, audience,* etc., may take either a singular or a plural verb, depending on their use in the sentence.

> *Examples*: *The <u>staff</u> <u>is</u> in a meeting.*
>
> *Staff is acting as a unit.*
>
> *The <u>couple</u> <u>disagree</u> about disciplining their child.*
>
> *The couple refers to two people who are acting as individuals.*

NOTE

Anyone who uses a plural verb with a collective noun must take care to be accurate—and also consistent. It must not be done carelessly. The following is the sort of flawed sentence one sees and hears a lot these days:

The staff is deciding how they want to vote.
Careful speakers and writers would avoid assigning the singular *is* and the plural *they* to *staff* in the same sentence.

Consistent: *The staff **are** deciding how **they** want to vote.*

Rewriting such sentences is recommended whenever possible. The preceding sentence would read even better as:

The staff members are deciding how they want to vote.

Rule 10. The word *were* replaces *was* in sentences that express a wish or are contrary to fact:

> *Example*: *If Joe **were** here, you'd be sorry.*

Shouldn't *Joe* be followed by *was*, not *were*, given that *Joe* is singular? But Joe isn't actually here, so we say *were*, not *was*. The sentence demonstrates the **subjunctive mood**, which is used to express things that are hypothetical, wishful, imaginary, or factually contradictory. The subjunctive mood pairs singular subjects with what we usually think of as plural verbs.

> *Examples*: *I wish it **were** Friday.*
>
> *She requested that he **raise** his hand.*

In the first example, a wishful statement, not a fact, is being expressed; therefore, *were*, which we usually think of as a plural verb, is used with the singular subject *I*.

Normally, *he raise* would sound terrible to us. However, in the second example, where a request is being expressed, the subjunctive mood is correct.

Note: The subjunctive mood is losing ground in spoken English but should still be used in formal speech and writing.

CLAUSES AND PHRASES

Definitions

- A **clause** is a group of words containing a subject and verb. An **independent clause** is a simple sentence. It can stand on its own.
  Examples: *She is hungry.*
  I am feeling well today.

- A **dependent clause** cannot stand on its own. It needs an independent clause to complete a sentence. Dependent clauses often begin with such words as *although, since, if, when,* and *because.*

  Examples: *Although she is hungry. . .*
  Whoever is hungry. . .
  Because I am feeling well. . .

Dependent	Independent
Although she is hungry,	*she will give him some of her food.*
Whatever they decide,	*I will agree to.*

- A **phrase** is a group of words without a subject-verb component, used as a single part of speech.

  Examples: *Best friend* (noun phrase)
  Needing help (adjective phrase; see the "Adjectives and Adverbs" section later in this chapter)
  With the blue shirt (prepositional adjective phrase; see the "Prepositions" section later in this chapter)
  For twenty days (prepositional adverb phrase)

PRONOUNS

Definition

- A **pronoun** (*I, me, he, she, herself, you, it, that, they, each, few, many, who, whoever, whose, someone, everybody,* etc.) is a word that takes the place of a noun. In the sentence *Joe saw Jill, and he waved at her,* the pronouns *he* and *her* take the place of *Joe* and

Jill, respectively. There are three types of pronouns: **subject** (for example, *he*); **object** (*him*); or **possessive** (*his*).

Rule 1. Subject pronouns are used when the pronoun is the subject of the sentence. You can remember subject pronouns easily by filling in the blank subject space for a simple sentence.

> **Example**:   ____ *did the job*.

I, he, she, we, they, who, whoever, etc., all qualify and are, therefore, subject pronouns.

Rule 2. Subject pronouns are also used if they rename the subject. They will follow *to be* verbs, such as *is, are, was, were, am, will be, had been*, etc.

> **Examples**:   *It is he.*
> *This is she speaking.*
> *It is we who are responsible for the decision to downsize.*

NOTE

In informal English, most people tend to follow *to be* verbs with object pronouns like *me, her, them*. Many English scholars tolerate this distinction between formal and casual English.

Example:	*It could have been them.*
Technically correct:	*It could have been **they**.*
Example:	*It is just me at the door.*
Technically correct:	*It is just **I** at the door.*

Rule 3. This rule surprises even language watchers: when *who* refers to a personal pronoun (*I, you, he, she, we, they*), it takes the verb that agrees with that pronoun.

> **Correct**:   *It is I who **am** sorry.* (*I **am***)
> **Incorrect**:   *It is I who is sorry.*
> **Correct**:   *It is you who **are** mistaken.* (*you **are***)
> **Incorrect**:   *It is you who's mistaken.*

Rule 4. Object pronouns are used everywhere else beyond Rules 1 and 2 (**direct object, indirect object, object of a preposition**). Object pronouns include *me, him, herself, us, them, themselves*, etc.

> **Examples**:   *Jean saw **him**.*
> *Him is the direct object.*
> *Give **her** the book.*
> *Her is the indirect object. The direct object is book.*
> *Are you talking to **me**?*
> *Me is the object of the preposition to.*

Rule 5. The pronouns *who, that*, and *which* become singular or plural depending on the subject. If the subject is singular, use a singular verb. If it is plural, use a plural verb.

> *Example*:   *He is the only one of those men who is always on time.*
> The word *who* refers to *one*. Therefore, use the singular verb *is*.

Sometimes we must look more closely to find a verb's true subject:

> *Example*:   *He is one of those men who **are** always on time.*
> The word *who* refers to *men*. Therefore, use the plural verb *are*.

In sentences like this last example, many would mistakenly insist that *one* is the subject, requiring **is** *always on time*. But look at it this way: *Of those men who **are** always on time, he is one.*

Rule 6. Pronouns that are singular (*I, he, she, everyone, everybody, anyone, anybody, no one, nobody, someone, somebody, each, either, neither*, etc.) require singular verbs. This rule is frequently overlooked when using the pronouns *each, either*, and *neither*, followed by *of*. Those three pronouns always take singular verbs. Do not be misled by what follows *of*.

> *Examples*:   *Each of the girls sings well.*
> *Either of us is capable of doing the job.*
> *Neither of them is available to speak right now.*

Exception: When *each* follows a noun or pronoun in certain sentences, even experienced writers sometimes get tripped up:

> *Incorrect*:   *The women each gave her approval.*
> *Correct*:   *The women each gave their approval.*
> *Incorrect*:   *The words are and there each ends with a silent vowel.*
> *Correct*:   *The words are and there each end with a silent vowel.*

These examples do not contradict Rule 6, because *each* is not the subject, but rather an **adjunct** describing the true subject.

Rule 7. To decide whether to use the subject or object pronoun after the words *than* or *as*, mentally complete the sentence.

> *Examples*:   *Tranh is as smart as she/her.*
> If we mentally complete the sentence, we would say *Tranh is as smart as she is*. Therefore, *she* is the correct answer.
> *Zoe is taller than I/me.*
> Mentally completing the sentence, we have *Zoe is taller than I am.*
> *Daniel would rather talk to her than I/me.*
> We can interpret this sentence in two ways: *Daniel would rather talk to her than to me.* **OR** *Daniel would rather talk to her than I would.* A sentence's meaning can change considerably, depending on the pronoun you choose.

Rule 8. The possessive pronouns *yours, his, hers, its, ours, theirs,* and *whose* never need apostrophes. Avoid mistakes like *her's* and *your's*.

Rule 9. The only time *it's* has an apostrophe is when it is a contraction for *it is* or *it has*. The only time *who's* has an apostrophe is when it means *who is* or *who has*. There is no apostrophe in *oneself*. Avoid "one's self," a common error.

Examples:	*It's been a cold morning.*
	The thermometer reached its highest reading.
	He's the one who's always on time.
	He's the one whose wife is always on time.
	Keeping oneself ready is important.

Rule 10. Pronouns that end in *-self* or *-selves* are called **reflexive pronouns**. There are nine reflexive pronouns: *myself, yourself, himself, herself, itself, oneself, ourselves, yourselves,* and *themselves*.

Reflexive pronouns are used when both the subject and the object of a verb are the same person or thing.

Example: *Joe helped* **himself**.

If the object of a preposition refers to a previous noun or pronoun, use a reflexive pronoun:

Example: *Joe bought it for himself.*

Reflexive pronouns help avoid confusion and nonsense. Without them, we might be stuck with sentences like *Joe helped Joe.*

Correct:	*I worked myself to the bone.*
	The object *myself* is the same person as the subject *I*, performing the act of working.
Incorrect:	*My brother and myself did it.*
Correct:	*My brother and I did it.*
	Don't use *myself* unless the pronoun *I* or *me* precedes it in the sentence.
Incorrect:	*Please give it to John or myself.*
Correct:	*Please give it to John or me.*
Correct:	*You saw me being myself.*
	Myself refers back to *me* in the act of being.

A sentence like *Help yourself* looks like an exception to the rule until we realize it's shorthand for **You** *may help yourself.*

In certain cases, a reflexive pronoun may come first.

Example: *Doubting himself, the man proceeded cautiously.*

Reflexive pronouns are also used for emphasis.

Example: *He himself finished the whole job.*

Rule 11a. Avoid *they* and *their* with singular pronouns.

Incorrect:	*Someone brought their lunch.*
Correct:	*Someone brought **her** lunch.*
	OR
	*Someone brought **his** lunch.*

If the gender is undetermined, you could say *Someone brought **his or her** lunch* (more on this option in Rule 11b).

Rule 11b. Singular pronouns must stay singular throughout the sentence.

Incorrect: *Someone has to do it—and they have to do it well.*

The problem is that *someone* is singular, but *they* is plural. If we change *they* to *he or she*, we get a rather clumsy sentence, even if it is technically correct.

Technically correct: *Someone has to do it—and he or she has to do it well.*

Replacing an ungrammatical sentence with a poorly written correction is a bad bargain. The better option is to rewrite.

Rewritten: *Someone has to do it—and has to do it well.*

Many writers abhor the *he or she* solution. Following are more examples of why rewriting is a better idea than using *he or she* or *him or her* to make sentences grammatical.

Incorrect:	*No one realizes when their time is up.*
Correct but awkward:	*No one realizes when his or her time is up.*
Rewritten:	*None realize when their time is up.*
Incorrect:	*If you see anyone on the trail, tell them to be careful.*
Correct but awkward:	*If you see anyone on the trail, tell him or her to be careful.*
Rewritten:	*Tell anyone you see on the trail to be careful.*

Rule 12. When a pronoun is linked with a noun by *and*, mentally remove the *and* + noun phrase to avoid trouble.

Incorrect:	*Her and her friend came over.*
	If we remove *and her friend*, we're left with the ungrammatical *Her came over.*
Correct:	***She** and her friend came over.*

Incorrect: *I invited he and his wife.*

             If we remove *and his wife*, we're left with the ungrammatical *I invited he.*

Correct: *I invited **him** and his wife.*

Incorrect: *Bill asked my sister and I.*

             If we remove *my sister and*, we're left with the ungrammatical *Bill asked I.*

Correct: *Bill asked my sister and **me**.*

NOTE

Do not combine a subject pronoun and an object pronoun in phrases like *her and I* or *he and me*. Whenever *and* or *or* links an object pronoun (*her, me*) and a subject pronoun (*he, I*), one of those pronouns will always be wrong.

Incorrect: *Her and I went home.*

Correct: *She and I went home.* (She went and I went.)

WHO VS. WHOM

Rule. Use this *he/him* method to decide whether *who* or *whom* is correct:

he = who

him = whom

Examples: **Who**/Whom *wrote the letter?*

             He wrote the letter. Therefore, *who* is correct.

             *Who/**Whom** should I vote for?*

             Should I vote for *him*? Therefore, *whom* is correct.

             *We all know **who**/whom pulled that prank.*

             This sentence contains two clauses: *we all know* and *who/whom pulled that prank*. We are interested in the second clause because it contains the *who/whom*. *He* pulled that prank. Therefore, *who* is correct.

             *We wondered who/**whom** the book was about.*

             This sentence contains two clauses: *we wondered* and *who/whom the book was about*. Again, we are interested in the second clause because it contains the *who/whom*. The book was about *him*. Therefore, *whom* is correct.

Note: This rule is compromised by an odd infatuation people have with *whom*—and not for good reasons. At its worst, the use of *whom* becomes a form of one-upmanship some employ to appear sophisticated. The following is an example of the pseudo-sophisticated *whom*.

Incorrect: *a woman whom I think is a genius*
              In this case *whom* is not the object of *I think*. Put *I think* at the end and witness the folly: *a woman whom is a genius, I think.*

Correct: *a woman **who** I think is a genius*

Learn to spot and avoid this too-common pitfall.

WHOEVER VS. WHOMEVER

To determine whether to use *whoever* or *whomever*, the *he/him* rule in the previous section applies:

he = whoever

him = whomever

Rule 1. The presence of *whoever* or *whomever* indicates a dependent clause. Use *whoever* or *whomever* to agree with the verb in that dependent clause, regardless of the rest of the sentence.

Examples: *Give it to **whoever**/whomever asks for it first.*
              He asks for it first. Therefore, *whoever* is correct.
              *We will hire whoever/**whomever** you recommend.*
              You recommend *him*. Therefore, *whomever* is correct.
              *We will hire **whoever**/whomever is most qualified.*
              He is most qualified. Therefore, *whoever* is correct.

Rule 2. When the entire *whoever/whomever* clause is the subject of the verb that follows the clause, analyze the clause to determine whether to use *whoever* or *whomever*.

Examples: *Whoever is elected will serve a four-year term.*
              Whoever is the subject of *is elected*. The clause *whoever is elected* is the subject of *will serve*.
              Whomever you elect will serve a four-year term.
              Whomever is the object of *elect*. *Whomever you elect* is the subject of *will serve*.

A word to the wise: *Whomever* is even more of a vogue word than *whom*. Many use it indiscriminately to sound cultured, figuring that no one will know any better.

WHO, THAT, WHICH

Rule 1. *Who* and sometimes *that* refer to people. *That* and *which* refer to groups or things.

Examples: *Anya is the one **who** rescued the bird.*
*"The Man **That** Got Away" is a great song with a grammatical title.*
*Lokua is on the team **that** won first place.*
*She belongs to a great organization, **which** specializes in saving endangered species.*

Rule 2a. *That* introduces what is called an **essential clause**. Essential clauses add information that is vital to the point of the sentence.

Example: *I do not trust products **that** claim "all natural ingredients" because this phrase can mean almost anything.*
We would not know the type of products being discussed without the *that* clause.

Rule 2b. *Which* introduces a **nonessential clause**, which adds supplementary information.

Example: *The product claiming "all natural ingredients," **which** appeared in the Sunday newspaper, is on sale.*
The product is already identified. Therefore, *which* begins a nonessential clause containing additional, but not essential, information.

NOTE
Essential clauses do not have commas introducing or surrounding them, whereas nonessential clauses are introduced or surrounded by commas.

Rule 3. If *that* has already appeared in a sentence, writers sometimes use *which* to introduce the next clause, whether it is essential or nonessential. This is done to avoid awkward formations.

Example: *That which doesn't kill you makes you stronger.*

This sentence is far preferable to the ungainly but technically correct *That that doesn't kill you makes you stronger.*

NOTE

The distinction between *that* and *which*, though a useful guideline, is widely disregarded: *Which* is routinely used in place of *that*, even by great writers and journalists, perhaps because it sounds more elegant.

ADJECTIVES AND ADVERBS

Definitions

- An **adjective** is a word or set of words that **modifies** (i.e., describes) a noun or pronoun. Adjectives may come before the word they modify.

  Examples: *That is a **cute** puppy.*
  *She likes a **high school** senior.*

Adjectives may also follow the word they modify:

Examples: *That puppy looks **cute**.*
*The technology is **state-of-the-art**.*

- An **adverb** is a word or set of words that modifies verbs, adjectives, or other adverbs.

  Examples: *He speaks **slowly*** (modifies the verb *speaks*)
  *He is **especially** clever* (modifies the adjective *clever*)
  *He speaks **all too** slowly* (modifies the adverb *slowly*)

An adverb answers how, when, where, or to what extent—how often or how much (e.g., *daily, completely*).

Examples: *He speaks **slowly*** (answers the question *how*)
*He speaks **very** slowly* (answers the question *how slowly*)

Rule 1. Many adverbs end in *-ly*, but many do not. Generally, if a word can have *-ly* added to its adjective form, place it there to form an adverb.

> *Examples*:   *She thinks quick/**quickly**.*
> How does she think? *Quickly*.
> *She is a **quick**/quickly thinker.*
> *Quick* is an adjective describing *thinker*, so no *-ly* is attached.
> *She thinks **fast**/fastly.*
> *Fast* answers the question *how*, so it is an adverb. But *fast* never has *-ly* attached to it.
> *We performed bad/**badly**.*
> *Badly* describes *how* we performed, so *-ly* is added.

Rule 2. Adverbs that answer the question *how* sometimes cause grammatical problems. It can be a challenge to determine if *-ly* should be attached. Avoid the trap of *-ly* with linking verbs, such as *taste, smell, look, feel*, etc., that pertain to the senses. Adverbs are often misplaced in such sentences, which require adjectives instead.

> *Examples*:   *Roses smell **sweet**/sweetly.*
> Do the roses actively smell with noses? No; in this case, *smell* is a linking verb—which requires an adjective to modify *roses*—so no *-ly*.
> *The woman looked **angry**/angrily to us.*
> Did the woman look with her eyes, or are we describing her appearance? We are describing her appearance (she appeared angry), so no *-ly*.
> *The woman looked angry/**angrily** at the paint splotches.*
> Here the woman actively looked (used her eyes), so the *-ly* is added.
> *She feels **bad**/badly about the news.*
> She is not feeling with fingers, so no *-ly*.

Rule 3. The word *good* is an adjective, whose adverb equivalent is *well*.

> *Examples*:   *You did a good job.*
> *Good* describes the job.
> *You did the job well.*
> *Well* answers *how*.
> *You smell good today.*
> *Good* describes your fragrance, not how you smell with your nose, so using the adjective is correct.
> *You smell well for someone with a cold.*
> You are actively smelling with your nose here, so use the adverb.

Rule 4. The word *well* can be an adjective, too. When referring to health, we often use *well* rather than *good*.

> ***Examples***:   *You do not look well today.*
> *I don't feel well, either.*

Rule 5. Adjectives come in three forms, also called **degrees**. An adjective in its normal or usual form is called a **positive degree adjective**. There are also the **comparative** and **superlative** degrees, which are used for comparison, as in the following examples:

Positive	Comparative	Superlative
sweet	*sweeter*	*sweetest*
bad	*worse*	*worst*
efficient	*more efficient*	*most efficient*

A common error in using adjectives and adverbs arises from using the wrong form of comparison. To compare two things, always use a **comparative** adjective:

> ***Example***:   *She is the **cleverer** of the two women* (never *cleverest*)

The word *cleverest* is what is called the **superlative** form of *clever*. Use it only when comparing three or more things:

> ***Example***:   *She is the **cleverest** of them all.*

> ***Incorrect***:   *Chocolate or vanilla: which do you like best?*
> ***Correct***:   *Chocolate or vanilla: which do you like **better**?*

Rule 6. There are also three degrees of adverbs. In formal usage, do not drop the *-ly* from an adverb when using the comparative form.

> ***Incorrect***:   *She spoke quicker than he did.*
> ***Correct***:   *She spoke **more quickly** than he did.*
> ***Incorrect***:   *Talk quieter.*
> ***Correct***:   *Talk **more quietly**.*

Rule 7. When *this, that, these,* and *those* are followed by a noun, they are adjectives. When they appear without a noun following them, they are pronouns.

> ***Examples***:   *This house is for sale.*
> *This is an adjective.*
> *This is for sale.*
> *This is a pronoun.*

PREPOSITIONS

Definition

- A **preposition** is a word that indicates location (*in, near, beside*) or some other relationship (*about, after, besides*) between a noun or pronoun and other parts of the sentence. A preposition isn't a preposition unless it goes with a related noun or pronoun, called the **object of the preposition**.

Examples: *Let's meet before noon.*
         Before is a preposition; *noon* is its object.
         We've never met before.
         There is no object; *before* is an adverb modifying *met.*

Rule 1. A preposition generally, but not always, goes before its noun or pronoun. One of the undying myths of English grammar is that you may not end a sentence with a preposition. But look at the first example that follows. No one should feel compelled to say, or even write, *That is something with which I cannot agree.* Just do not use extra prepositions when the meaning is clear without them.

Correct: *That is something I cannot agree* **with**.
Correct: *Where did you get this?*
Incorrect: *Where did you get this* **at**?
Correct: *How many of you can I depend* **on**?
Correct: *Where did he go?*
Incorrect: *Where did he go* **to**?

Rule 2a. The preposition *like* means "similar to" or "similarly to." It should be followed by an object of the preposition (noun, pronoun, noun phrase), not by a subject and verb. Rule of thumb: Avoid *like* when a verb is involved.

Correct: *You look like your mother.*
         That is, you look *similar to* her. (*Mother* is the object of the preposition *like*.)
Incorrect: *You look like your mother does.*
         (Avoid *like* with noun + verb.)

Rule 2b. Instead of *like*, use *as, as if, as though*, or *the way* when following a comparison with a subject and verb.

Correct:	*You look **the way** your mother does.*
Incorrect:	*Do like I ask.* (No one would say *Do similarly to I ask.*)
Correct:	*Do **as** I ask.*
Incorrect:	*You look like you're angry.*
Correct:	*You look **as if** you're angry.* (**OR as though**)

Some speakers and writers, to avoid embarrassment, use *as* when they mean *like*. The following incorrect sentence came from a grammar guide:

Incorrect:	*They are considered as any other English words.*
Correct:	*They are considered as any other English words would be.*
Correct:	*They are considered to be like any other English words.*

Remember: *like* means "similar to" or "similarly to"; *as* means "in the same manner that." Rule of thumb: Do not use *as* unless there is a verb involved.

Incorrect:	*I, as most people, try to use good grammar.*
Correct:	*I, **like** most people, try to use good grammar.*
Correct:	*I, **as** most people **do**, try to use good grammar.*

NOTE

The rule distinguishing *like* from *as, as if, as though*, and *the way* is increasingly ignored, but English purists still insist upon it.

Rule 3. The preposition *of* should never be used in place of the helping verb *have*.

Correct:	*I should have done it.*
Incorrect:	*I should of done it.*

Rule 4. Follow *different* with the preposition *from*. Things differ *from* other things; avoid *different than*.

Incorrect:	*You're different than I am.*
Correct:	*You're different from me.*

Rule 5. Use *into* rather than *in* to express motion toward something. Use *in* to tell the location.

Correct:	*I swam in the pool.*
Correct:	*I walked into the house.*
Correct:	*I looked into the matter.*
Incorrect:	*I dived in the water.*
Correct:	*I dived into the water.*
Incorrect:	*Throw it in the trash.*
Correct:	*Throw it into the trash.*

EFFECTIVE WRITING

Rule 1. Use concrete rather than vague language.

Vague:	*The weather was of an extreme nature on the West Coast.*
	This sentence raises frustrating questions: When did this extreme weather occur? What does "of an extreme nature" mean? Where on the West Coast did this take place?
Concrete:	*California had unusually cold weather last week.*

Rule 2. Use **active voice** whenever possible. Active voice means the subject is performing the verb. **Passive voice** means the subject receives the action.

Active:	*Barry hit the ball.*
Passive:	*The ball was hit.*

Notice that the party responsible for the action—in the previous example, whoever hit the ball—may not even appear when using passive voice. So passive voice is a useful option when the responsible party is not known.

Example:	*My watch was stolen.*

NOTE
The passive voice has often been criticized as something employed by people in power to avoid responsibility:

Example:	*Mistakes were made.*
Translation:	*I made mistakes.*

Rule 3. Avoid overusing *there is, there are, it is, it was*, etc.

> *Example*:   *There is a case of meningitis that was reported in the newspaper.*
> *Revision*:   *A case of meningitis was reported in the newspaper.*
> *Even better*:   *The newspaper reported a case of meningitis.* (Active voice)

> *Example*:   *It is important to signal before making a left turn.*
> *Revision*:   *Signaling before making a left turn is important.*
> **OR**
> *Signaling before a left turn is important.*
> **OR**
> *You should signal before making a left turn.*

> *Example*:   *There are some revisions that must be made.*
> *Revision*:   *Some revisions must be made.* (Passive voice)
> *Even better*:   *Please make some revisions.* (Active voice)

Rule 4. To avoid confusion (and pompousness), don't use two negatives to make a positive without good reason.

> *Unnecessary*:   *He is not unwilling to help.*
> *Better*:   *He is willing to help.*

Sometimes a *not un-* construction may be desirable, perhaps even necessary:

Example: *The book is uneven but not uninteresting.*

However, the novelist-essayist George Orwell warned of its abuse with this deliberately silly sentence: "A not unblack dog was chasing a not unsmall rabbit across a not ungreen field."

Rule 5. Use consistent grammatical form when offering several ideas. This is called **parallel construction**.

> *Correct*:   *I admire people who are honest, reliable, and sincere.*
> Note that *are* applies to and makes sense with each of the three adjectives at the end.
> *Incorrect*:   *I admire people who are honest, reliable, and have sincerity.*
> In this version, *are* does not make sense with *have sincerity*, and *have sincerity* doesn't belong with the two adjectives *honest* and *reliable*.

Correct: *You should check your spelling, grammar, and punctuation.*
              Note that *check your* applies to and makes sense with each
                    of the three nouns at the end.
Incorrect: *You should check your spelling, grammar, and punctuate*
                    properly.
              Here, *check your* does not make sense with *punctuate*
                    properly, and *punctuate properly* doesn't belong with the
                    two nouns *spelling* and *grammar*. The result is a
                    jarringly inept sentence.

Rule 6. Word order can make or ruin a sentence. If you start a sentence with an incomplete phrase or clause, such as *While crossing the street* or *Forgotten by history*, it must be followed closely by the person or thing it describes. Furthermore, that person or thing is always the main subject of the sentence. Breaking this rule results in the dreaded, all-too-common **dangling modifier**, or **dangler**.

Dangler: *Forgotten by history, his autograph was worthless.*
              The problem: *his autograph* shouldn't come right after
                    history, because *he* was forgotten, not his autograph.
Correct: *He was forgotten by history, and his autograph was*
                    worthless.
Dangler: *Born in Chicago, my first book was about the 1871 fire.*
              The problem: the sentence wants to say *I* was born in
                    Chicago, but to a careful reader, it says that *my first*
                    book was born there.
Correct: *I was born in Chicago, and my first book was about*
                    the 1871 fire.

Adding *-ing* to a verb (as in *crossing* in the example that follows) results in a versatile word called a **participle**, which can be a noun, adjective, or adverb. Rule 6 applies to all sentences with a participle in the beginning. Participles require placing the actor immediately after the opening phrase or clause.

Dangler: *While crossing the street, the bus hit her.* (Wrong: the bus was not crossing.)
Correct: *While crossing the street, she was hit by a bus.*
              OR
              She was hit by a bus while crossing the street.

Rule 7. Place descriptive words and phrases as close as is practical to the words they modify.

Ill-advised: *I have a cake that Mollie baked in my lunch bag.*

Cake is too far from *lunch bag*, making the sentence ambiguous and silly.

Better: *In my lunch bag is a cake that Mollie baked.*

Rule 8. A sentence fragment is usually an oversight, or a bad idea. It occurs when you have only a phrase or dependent clause but are missing an independent clause.

Sentence fragment: *After the show ended.*

Full sentence: *After the show ended, we had coffee.*

CHAPTER 2

PUNCTUATION

PERIODS

Rule 1. Use a period at the end of a complete sentence that is a statement.

    Example: *I know him well.*

Rule 2. If the last item in the sentence is an abbreviation that ends in a period, do not follow it with another period.

    Incorrect: *This is Alice Smith, M.D..*
    Correct: *This is Alice Smith, M.D.*
    Correct: *Please shop, cook, etc. We will do the laundry.*

Rule 3. Question marks and exclamation points replace and eliminate periods at the end of a sentence.

COMMAS

Commas and **periods** are the most frequently used punctuation marks. Commas customarily indicate a brief pause; they're not as final as periods.

Rule 1. Use commas to separate words and word groups in a simple series of three or more items.

    Example: *My estate goes to my husband, son, daughter-in-law, and nephew.*

Note: When the last comma in a series comes before *and* or *or* (after *daughter-in-law* in the above example), it is known as the **Oxford comma**. Most newspapers and magazines drop the Oxford comma in a simple series, apparently feeling it's unnecessary. However, omission of the Oxford comma can sometimes lead to misunderstandings.

> *Example*:   *We had coffee, cheese and crackers and grapes.*

Adding a comma after *crackers* makes it clear that *cheese and crackers* represents one dish. In cases like this, clarity demands the Oxford comma.

> *We had coffee, cheese and crackers, and grapes.*

Fiction and nonfiction books generally prefer the Oxford comma. Writers must decide Oxford or no Oxford and not switch back and forth, except when omitting the Oxford comma could cause confusion as in the *cheese and crackers* example.

Rule 2. Use a comma to separate two adjectives when the adjectives are interchangeable.

> *Example*:   *He is a strong, healthy man.*
> *We could also say* healthy, strong man.
> *Example*:   *We stayed at an expensive summer resort.*
> *We would not say* summer expensive resort, *so no comma.*

Rule 3a. Many inexperienced writers run two independent clauses together by using a comma instead of a period. This results in the dreaded **run-on sentence** or, more technically, a **comma splice**.

> *Incorrect*:   *He walked all the way home, he shut the door.*

There are several simple remedies:

> *Correct*:   *He walked all the way home. He shut the door.*
> *Correct*:   *After he walked all the way home, he shut the door.*
> *Correct*:   *He walked all the way home, and he shut the door.*

Rule 3b. In sentences where two independent clauses are joined by connectors such as *and, or, but*, etc., put a comma at the end of the first clause.

> *Incorrect*:   *He walked all the way home and he shut the door.*
> *Correct*:   *He walked all the way home, and he shut the door.*

Some writers omit the comma if the clauses are both quite short:

Example: *I paint and he writes.*

Rule 3c. If the subject does not appear in front of the second verb, a comma is generally unnecessary.

Example: *He <u>thought</u> quickly but still <u>did</u> not <u>answer</u> correctly.*

Rule 4a. Use a comma after certain words that introduce a sentence, such as *well, yes, why, hello, hey,* etc.

Examples: *Why, I can't believe this!*
              No, you can't have a dollar.

Rule 4b. Use commas to set off expressions that interrupt the sentence flow (*nevertheless, after all, by the way, on the other hand, however,* etc.).

Example: *I am, by the way, very nervous about this.*

Rule 5. Use commas to set off the name, nickname, term of endearment, or title of a person directly addressed.

Examples: *Will you, Aisha, do that assignment for me?*
              Yes, old friend, I will.
              Good day, Captain.

Rule 6. Use a comma to separate the day of the month from the year, and—what most people forget!—always put one after the year, also.

Example: *It was in the Sun's June 5, 2003, edition.*

No comma is necessary for just the month and year.

Example: *It was in a June 2003 article.*

Rule 7. Use a comma to separate a city from its state, and remember to put one after the state, also.

Example: *I'm from the Akron, Ohio, area.*

Rule 8. Traditionally, if a person's name is followed by *Sr.* or *Jr.*, a comma follows the last name: *Martin Luther King, Jr.* This comma is no longer considered mandatory. However, if a comma does precede *Sr.* or *Jr.*, another comma must follow the entire name when it appears midsentence.

Correct:	*Al Mooney Sr. is here.*
Correct:	*Al Mooney, Sr., is here.*
Incorrect:	*Al Mooney, Sr. is here.*

Rule 9. Similarly, use commas to enclose degrees or titles used with names.

Example: *Al Mooney, M.D., is here.*

Rule 10. When starting a sentence with a dependent clause, use a comma after it.

Example: *If you are not sure about this, let me know now.*

But often a comma is unnecessary when the sentence starts with an independent clause followed by a dependent clause.

Example: *Let me know now if you are not sure about this.*

Rule 11. Use commas to set off nonessential words, clauses, and phrases (see the "Who, That, Which" section in Chapter One, Rule 2b).

Incorrect:	*Jill who is my sister shut the door.*
Correct:	*Jill, who is my sister, shut the door.*
Incorrect:	*The man knowing it was late hurried home.*
Correct:	*The man, knowing it was late, hurried home.*

In the preceding examples, note the comma after *sister* and *late*. Nonessential words, clauses, and phrases that occur midsentence must be enclosed by commas. The closing comma is called an **appositive comma**. Many writers forget to add this important comma. Following are two instances of the need for an appositive comma with one or more nouns.

Incorrect:	*My best friend, Joe arrived.*
Correct:	*My best friend, Joe, arrived.*
Incorrect:	*The three items, a book, a pen, and paper were on the table.*
Correct:	*The three items, a book, a pen, and paper, were on the table.*

Rule 12. If something or someone is sufficiently identified, the description that follows is considered nonessential and should be surrounded by commas.

Examples: *Freddy, who has a limp, was in an auto accident.*
        If we already know which Freddy is meant, the description is not essential.
        The boy who has a limp was in an auto accident.
        We do not know which boy is meant without further description; therefore, no commas are used.

This leads to a persistent problem. Look at the following sentence:

Example:　*My brother Bill is here.*

Now, see how adding two commas changes that sentence's meaning:

Example:　*My brother, Bill, is here.*

Careful writers and readers understand that the first sentence means I have more than one brother. The commas in the second sentence mean that Bill is my only brother.

Why? In the first sentence, *Bill* is essential information: it identifies which of my two (or more) brothers I'm speaking of. This is why no commas enclose *Bill*.

In the second sentence, *Bill* is nonessential information—whom else but Bill could I mean?—hence the commas.

Comma misuse is nothing to take lightly. It can lead to a train wreck like this:

Example:　*Mark Twain's book*, Tom Sawyer, *is a delight.*

Because of the commas, that sentence states that Twain wrote only one book. In fact, he wrote more than two dozen of them.

Rule 13a. Use commas to introduce or interrupt direct quotations.

Examples:　*He said, "I don't care."*
　　　　　　"Why," I asked, "don't you care?"

This rule is optional with one-word quotations.

Example:　*He said "Stop."*

Rule 13b. If the quotation comes before *he said, she wrote, they reported, Dana insisted,* or a similar attribution, end the quoted material with a comma, even if it is only one word.

Examples:　*"I don't care," he said.*
　　　　　　"Stop," he said.

Rule 14. Use a comma to separate a statement from a question.

Example:　*I can go, can't I?*

Rule 15. Use a comma to separate contrasting parts of a sentence.

Example:　*That is my money, not yours.*

Rule 16a. Use a comma before and after certain introductory words or terms, such as *namely, that is, i.e., e.g.,* and *for instance,* when they are followed by a series of items.

Example: *You may be required to bring many items, e.g., sleeping bags, pans, and warm clothing.*

Rule 16b. Commas should precede the term *etc.* and enclose it if it is placed midsentence.

Example: *Sleeping bags, pans, warm clothing, etc., are in the tent.*

NOTE

The abbreviation *i.e.* means "that is"; *e.g.* means "for example."

SEMICOLONS

It's no accident that a **semicolon** is a period atop a comma. Like commas, semicolons indicate an audible pause—slightly longer than a comma's, but short of a period's full stop.

Semicolons have other functions, too. But first, a caveat: avoid the common mistake of using a semicolon to replace a colon (see the "Colons" section).

Incorrect: *I have one goal; to find her.*
Correct: *I have one goal: to find her.*

Rule 1. A semicolon can replace a period if the writer wishes to narrow the gap between two closely linked sentences.

Examples: *Call me tomorrow; you can give me an answer then.*
                We have paid our dues; we expect all the privileges listed in the contract.

Rule 2. Use a semicolon before such words and terms as *namely, however, therefore, that is, i.e., for example, e.g., for instance*, etc., when they introduce a complete sentence. It is also preferable to use a comma after these words and terms.

Example: *Bring any two items; however, sleeping bags and tents are in short supply.*

Rule 3. Use a semicolon to separate units of a series when one or more of the units contain commas.

Incorrect: *The conference has people who have come from Moscow, Idaho, Springfield, California, Alamo, Tennessee, and other places as well.*
                Note that with only commas, that sentence is hopeless.

Correct: *The conference has people who have come from Moscow, Idaho;*
               Springfield, California; Alamo, Tennessee; and other places as well.

Rule 4. A semicolon may be used between independent clauses joined by a connector, such as *and, but, or, nor*, etc., when one or more commas appear in the first clause.

Example: *When I finish here, and I will soon, I'll be glad to help you; and that is a*
               promise I will keep.

COLONS

A **colon** means "that is to say" or "here's what I mean." Colons and semicolons should never be used interchangeably.

Rule 1. Use a colon to introduce a series of items. Do not capitalize the first item after the colon (unless it's a proper noun).

Examples: *You may be required to bring many things: sleeping bags, pans, utensils,*
               and warm clothing.
               I want the following items: butter, sugar, and flour.
               I need an assistant who can do the following: input data, write reports,
               and complete tax forms.

Rule 2. Avoid using a colon before a list when it directly follows a verb or preposition.

Incorrect: *I want: butter, sugar, and flour.*
Correct: *I want the following: butter, sugar, and flour.*
               OR
               I want butter, sugar, and flour.
Incorrect: *I've seen the greats, including: Barrymore, Guinness, and Streep.*
Correct: *I've seen the greats, including Barrymore, Guinness, and Streep.*

Rule 3. When listing items one by one, one per line, following a colon, capitalization and ending punctuation are optional when using single words or phrases preceded by letters, numbers, or bullet points. If each point is a complete sentence, capitalize the first word and end the sentence with appropriate ending punctuation. Otherwise, there are no hard and fast rules, except be consistent.

Examples: I want an assistant who can do the following:

> (a) input data
> (b) write reports
> (c) complete tax forms

The following are requested:

- Wool sweaters for possible cold weather.

- Wet suits for snorkeling.

- Introductions to the local dignitaries.

These are the pool rules:

1. Do not run.
2. If you see unsafe behavior, report it to the lifeguard.
3. Did you remember your towel?
4. Have fun!

Rule 4. A colon instead of a semicolon may be used between independent clauses when the second sentence explains, illustrates, paraphrases, or expands on the first sentence.

Example: *He got what he worked for: he really earned that promotion.*

If a complete sentence follows a colon, as in the previous example, it is up to the writer to decide whether to capitalize the first word. Although generally advisable, capitalizing a sentence after a colon is often a judgment call.

Note: A capital letter generally does not introduce a simple phrase following a colon.

Example: *He got what he worked for: a promotion.*

Rule 5. A colon may be used to introduce a long quotation. Some style manuals say to indent one-half inch on both the left and right margins; others say to indent only on the left margin. Quotation marks are not used.

Example: *The author of* Touched, *Jane Straus, wrote in the first chapter:*
> *Georgia went back to her bed and stared at the intricate patterns of*
> *burned moth wings in the translucent glass of the overhead light.*
> *Her father was in "hyper mode" again where nothing could calm*
> *him down.*

Rule 6. Use a colon rather than a comma to follow the salutation in a business letter, even when addressing someone by his or her first name. (Never use a semicolon after a salutation.) A comma is used after the salutation in more informal correspondence.

Formal: *Dear Ms. Rodriguez:*
Informal: *Dear Dave,*

QUOTATION MARKS

The rules set forth in this section are customary in the United States. Great Britain and other countries in the Commonwealth of Nations are governed by quite different conventions. Nowhere is this more apparent than in Rule 3a in this section, a rule that has the advantage of being far simpler than Britain's and the disadvantage of being far less logical.

Rule 1. Use double quotation marks to set off a direct (word-for-word) quotation.

> *Correct*:   *"When will you be here?" he asked.*
> *Incorrect*:   *He asked "when I would be there."*

Rule 2. Either quotation marks or italics are customary for titles: magazines, books, plays, films, songs, poems, article titles, chapter titles, etc.

Rule 3a. Periods and commas ALWAYS go inside quotation marks.

> *Examples*:   *The sign said, "Walk." Then it said, "Don't Walk," then, "Walk," all within thirty seconds.*
> *He yelled, "Hurry up."*

Rule 3b. Use single quotation marks for quotations within quotations.

> *Example*:   *He said, "Dan cried, 'Do not treat me that way.' "*

Note that the period goes inside both the single and double quotation marks.

Rule 4. As a courtesy, make sure there is visible space at the start or end of a quotation between adjacent single and double quotation marks. (Your word processing program may do this automatically.)

> *Not ample space*:   *He said, "Dan cried, 'Do not treat me that way.'"*
> *Ample space*:   *He said, "Dan cried, 'Do not treat me that way.' "*

Rule 5a. Quotation marks are often used with technical terms, terms used in an unusual way, or other expressions that vary from standard usage.

> *Examples*:   *It's an oil-extraction method known as "fracking."*
> *He did some "experimenting" in his college days.*
> *I had a visit from my "friend" the tax man.*

Rule 5b. Never use single quotation marks in sentences like the previous three.

> *Incorrect*:   *I had a visit from my 'friend' the tax man.*

The single quotation marks in the above sentence are intended to send a message to the reader that *friend* is being used in a special way: in this case, sarcastically. Avoid this invalid usage. Single quotation marks are valid only within a quotation, as per Rule 3b, above.

Rule 6. When quoted material runs more than one paragraph, start each new paragraph with opening quotation marks, but do not use closing quotation marks until the end of the passage.

> *Example*:   *She wrote: "I don't paint anymore. For a while I thought it was just a*
> *phase that I'd get over.*
> *"Now, I don't even try."*

PARENTHESES AND BRACKETS

Parentheses and **brackets** must never be used interchangeably.

Parentheses

Rule 1. Use parentheses to enclose information that clarifies or is used as an aside.

> *Example*:   *He finally answered (after taking five minutes to think) that he did not*
> *understand the question.*

If material in parentheses ends a sentence, the period goes after the parentheses.

> *Example*:   *He gave me a nice bonus ($500).*

Commas could have been used in the first example; a colon could have been used in the second example. The use of parentheses indicates that the writer considered the information less important—almost an afterthought.

Rule 2. Periods go inside parentheses only if an entire sentence is inside the parentheses.

> *Example*:   *Please read the analysis. (You'll be amazed.)*

This is a rule with a lot of wiggle room. An entire sentence in parentheses is often acceptable without an enclosed period:

> *Example*:   *Please read the analysis (you'll be amazed).*

Rule 3. Parentheses, despite appearances, are not part of the subject.

> *Example*:   *Joe (and his trusty mutt)* **was** *always welcome.*

If this seems awkward, try rewriting the sentence:

> *Example*:   *Joe (accompanied by his trusty mutt)* **was** *always welcome.*

Rule 4. Commas are more likely to follow parentheses than precede them.

> *Incorrect*:   *When he got home, (it was already dark outside) he fixed dinner.*
> *Correct*:   *When he got home (it was already dark outside), he fixed dinner.*

Brackets

Brackets are far less common than parentheses, and they are only used in special cases. Brackets (like single quotation marks) are used exclusively within quoted material.

Rule 1. Brackets are interruptions. When we see them, we know they've been added by someone else. They are used to explain or comment on the quotation.

> *Examples*:   *"Four score and seven [today we'd say eighty-seven] years ago…"*
>   *"Bill shook hands with [his son] Al."*

Rule 2. When quoting something that has a spelling or grammar mistake or presents material in a confusing way, insert the term *sic* in italics and enclose it in nonitalic (unless the surrounding text is italic) brackets.

> *Sic* ("thus" in Latin) is shorthand for, "This is exactly what the original material says."

> *Example*:   *She wrote, "I would rather die then [sic] be seen wearing the same outfit*
>   *as my sister."*
>   The [sic] indicates that *then* was mistakenly used instead of *than*.

Rule 3. In formal writing, brackets are often used to maintain the integrity of both a quotation and the sentences others use it in.

> *Example*:   *"[T]he better angels of our nature" gave a powerful ending to Lincoln's*
>   *first inaugural address.*
>   Lincoln's memorable phrase came midsentence, so the word *the* was
>   not originally capitalized.

APOSTROPHES

Rule 1a. Use the **apostrophe** to show possession. To show possession with a singular noun, add an apostrophe plus the letter *s*.

> *Examples*:   *a woman's hat*
> *the boss's wife*
> *Mrs. Chang's house*

Rule 1b. Many common nouns end in the letter *s* (*lens, cactus, bus*, etc.). So do a lot of proper nouns (*Mr. Jones, Texas, Christmas*). There are conflicting policies and theories about how to show possession when writing such nouns. There is no right answer; the best advice is to choose a formula and stay consistent.

Rule 1c. Some writers and editors add only an apostrophe to all nouns ending in *s*. And some add an apostrophe + *s* to every proper noun, be it *Hastings's* or *Jones's*.

One method, common in newspapers and magazines, is to add an apostrophe + *s* ('*s*) to common nouns ending in *s*, but only a stand-alone apostrophe to proper nouns ending in *s*.

> *Examples*:   *the class's hours*
> *Mr. Jones' golf clubs*
> *the canvas's size*
> *Texas' weather*

Care must be taken to place the apostrophe outside the word in question. For instance, if talking about a pen belonging to Mr. Hastings, many people would wrongly write *Mr. Hasting's pen* (his name is not Mr. Hasting).

> *Correct*:   *Mr. Hastings' pen*

Another widely used technique is to write the word as we would speak it. For example, since most people saying, "Mr. Hastings' pen" would not pronounce an added *s*, we would write *Mr. Hastings' pen* with no added *s*. But most people would pronounce an added *s* in "Jones's," so we'd write it as we say it: *Mr. Jones's golf clubs*. This method explains the punctuation of *for goodness' sake*.

Rule 2a. **Regular nouns** are nouns that form their plurals by adding either the letter *s* or -*es* (*guy, guys; letter, letters; actress, actresses;* etc.). To show plural possession, simply put an apostrophe after the *s*.

> *Correct*:   *guys' night out* (*guy* + *s* + apostrophe)
> *Incorrect*:   *guy's night out* (implies only one guy)
> *Correct*:   *two actresses' roles* (*actress* + *es* + apostrophe)
> *Incorrect*:   *two actress's roles*

Rule 2b. Do not use an apostrophe + *s* to make a regular noun plural.

> ***Incorrect***:   *Apostrophe's are confusing.*
> ***Correct***:   *Apostrophes are confusing.*
> ***Incorrect***:   *We've had many happy Christmas's.*
> ***Correct***:   *We've had many happy Christmases.*

In special cases, such as when forming a plural of a word that is not normally a noun, some writers add an apostrophe for clarity.

> ***Example***:   *Here are some do's and don'ts.*

In that sentence, the verb *do* is used as a plural noun, and the apostrophe was added because the writer felt that *dos* was confusing. Not all writers agree; some see no problem with *dos and don'ts*.

Rule 2c. English also has many **irregular nouns** (*child, nucleus, tooth*, etc.). These nouns become plural by changing their spelling, sometimes becoming quite different words. You may find it helpful to write out the entire irregular plural noun before adding an apostrophe or an apostrophe + *s*.

> ***Incorrect***:   *two childrens' hats*
>   The plural is *children*, not *childrens*.
> ***Correct***:   *two children's hats* (*children* + apostrophe + *s*)
> ***Incorrect***:   *the teeths' roots*
> ***Correct***:   *the teeth's roots*

Rule 2d. Things can get really confusing with the possessive plurals of proper names ending in *s*, such as *Hastings* and *Jones*.

If you're the guest of the Ford family—the *Fords*—you're the *Fords'* guest (*Ford* + *s* + apostrophe). But what if it's the Hastings family?

Most would call them the "Hastings." But that would refer to a family named "Hasting." If someone's name ends in *s*, we must add *-es* for the plural. The plural of *Hastings* is *Hastingses*. The members of the Jones family are the *Joneses*.

To show possession, add an apostrophe.

> ***Incorrect***:   *the Hastings' dog*
> ***Correct***:   *the Hastingses' dog* (*Hastings* + *es* + apostrophe)
> ***Incorrect***:   *the Jones' car*
> ***Correct***:   *the Joneses' car*

In serious writing, this rule must be followed no matter how strange or awkward the results.

Rule 2e. Never use an apostrophe to make a name plural.

Incorrect:	*The Wilson's are here.*
Correct:	*The Wilsons are here.*
Incorrect:	*We visited the Sanchez's.*
Correct:	*We visited the Sanchezes.*

Rule 3. With a singular compound noun (for example, *mother-in-law*), show possession with an apostrophe + *s* at the end of the word.

Example: *my mother-in-law's hat*

If the compound noun (e.g., *brother-in-law*) is to be made plural, form the plural first (*brothers-in-law*), and then use the apostrophe + *s*.

Example: *my two brothers-in-law's hats*

Rule 4. If two people possess the same item, put the apostrophe + *s* after the second name only.

Example: *Cesar and Maribel's home is constructed of redwood.*

However, if one of the joint owners is written as a pronoun, use the possessive form for both.

Incorrect:	*Maribel and my home*
Correct:	*Maribel's and my home*
Incorrect:	*he and Maribel's home*
Incorrect:	*him and Maribel's home*
Correct:	*his and Maribel's home*

In cases of separate rather than joint possession, use the possessive form for both.

Examples:	*Cesar's and Maribel's homes are both lovely.*
	They don't own the homes jointly.
	Cesar and Maribel's homes are both lovely.
	The homes belong to both of them.

Rule 5. Use an apostrophe with **contractions**. The apostrophe is placed where a letter or letters have been removed.

Examples:	*doesn't, wouldn't, it's, can't, you've, etc.*
Incorrect:	*does'nt*

Rule 6. There are various approaches to plurals for initials, capital letters, and numbers used as nouns.

Examples: *She consulted with three M.D.s.*
She consulted with three M.D.'s.
Some write *M.D.'s* to give the *s* separation from the second period.

Many writers and editors prefer an apostrophe after single capital letters only:

Examples: *I made straight A's.*
He learned his ABCs.

There are different schools of thought about years and decades. The following examples are all in widespread use:

Examples: *the 1990s*
the 1990's
the '90s
the 90's
Awkward: *the '90's*

Rule 7. Amounts of time or money are sometimes used as possessive adjectives that require apostrophes.

Incorrect: *three days leave*
Correct: *three days' leave*
Incorrect: *my two cents worth*
Correct: *my two cents' worth*

Rule 8. The personal pronouns *hers, ours, yours, theirs, its, whose,* and *oneself* never take an apostrophe.

Example: *Feed a horse grain. It's better for its health.*

Rule 9. When an apostrophe comes before a word or number, take care that it's truly an apostrophe (') rather than a single quotation mark (').

Incorrect: *'Twas the night before Christmas.*
Correct: *'Twas the night before Christmas.*
Incorrect: *I voted in '08.*
Correct: *I voted in '08.*

NOTE
Serious writers avoid the word *'til* as an alternative to *until*. The correct word is *till*, which is many centuries older than *until*.

Rule 10. Beware of **false possessives**, which often occur with nouns ending in *s*. Don't add apostrophes to noun-derived adjectives ending in *s*. Close analysis is the best guide.

Incorrect: *We enjoyed the New Orleans' cuisine.*

In the preceding sentence, the word *the* makes no sense unless *New Orleans* is being used as an adjective to describe *cuisine*. In English, nouns frequently become adjectives. Adjectives rarely if ever take apostrophes.

Incorrect: *I like that Beatles' song.*
Correct: *I like that Beatles song.*

Again, *Beatles* is an adjective, modifying *song*.

Incorrect: *He's a United States' citizen.*
Correct: *He's a United States citizen.*

Rule 11. Beware of nouns ending in *y*; do not show possession by changing the *y* to *-ies*.

Correct: *the company's policy*
Incorrect: *the companies policy*
Correct: *three companies' policies*

HYPHENS

There are two commandments about this misunderstood punctuation mark. First, **hyphens** must never be used interchangeably with dashes (see the "Dashes" section), which are noticeably longer. Second, there should never be spaces around hyphens.

Incorrect: *300—325 people*
Incorrect: *300 - 325 people*
Correct: *300-325 people*

Hyphens' main purpose is to glue words together. They notify the reader that two or more elements in a sentence are linked. Although there are rules and customs governing hyphens, there are also situations when writers must decide whether to add them for clarity.

Hyphens Between Words

Rule 1. Generally, hyphenate two or more words when they come before a noun they modify and act as a single idea. This is called a **compound adjective**.

> *Examples*:   *an off-campus apartment*
> *state-of-the-art design*

When a compound adjective follows a noun, a hyphen may or may not be necessary.

> *Example*:   *The apartment is off campus.*

However, some established compound adjectives are always hyphenated. Double-check with a dictionary or online.

> *Example*:   *The design is state-of-the-art.*

Rule 2a. A hyphen is frequently required when forming original compound verbs for vivid writing, humor, or special situations.

> *Examples*:   *The slacker video-gamed his way through life.*
> *Queen Victoria throne-sat for six decades.*

Rule 2b. When writing out new, original, or unusual compound nouns, writers should hyphenate whenever doing so avoids confusion.

> *Examples*:   *I changed my diet and became a no-meater.*
> *No-meater* is too confusing without the hyphen.
> *The slacker was a video gamer.*
> *Video gamer* is clear without a hyphen, although some writers might
>   prefer to hyphenate it.

Writers using familiar compound verbs and nouns should consult a dictionary or look online to decide if these verbs and nouns should be hyphenated.

Rule 3. An often overlooked rule for hyphens: The adverb *very* and adverbs ending in *-ly* are not hyphenated.

> *Incorrect*:   *the very-elegant watch*
> *Incorrect*:   *the finely-tuned watch*

This rule applies only to adverbs. The following two sentences are correct because the *-ly* words are adjectives rather than adverbs:

> *Correct*:   *the friendly-looking dog*
> *Correct*:   *a family-owned cafe*

Rule 4. Hyphens are often used to tell the ages of people and things. A handy rule, whether writing about years, months, or any other period of time, is to use hyphens unless the period of time (years, months, weeks, days) is written in plural form:

With hyphens:	*We have a two-year-old child.*
	We have a two-year-old.
No hyphens:	*The child is two years old.* (Because *years* is plural.)
Exception:	*The child is one year old.* (Or *day, week, month,* etc.)

Note that when hyphens are involved in expressing ages, two hyphens are required. Many writers forget the second hyphen:

Incorrect:	*We have a two-year old child.*
	Without the second hyphen, the sentence is about an "old child."

Rule 5. Never hesitate to add a hyphen if it solves a possible problem. Following are two examples of well-advised hyphens:

Confusing:	*I have a few more important things to do.*
With hyphen:	*I have a few more-important things to do.*
	Without the hyphen, it's impossible to tell whether the sentence is about a *few things* that are *more important* or a few more things that are all equally important.
Confusing:	*He returned the stolen vehicle report.*
With hyphen:	*He returned the stolen-vehicle report.*
	With no hyphen, we could only guess: Was the *vehicle report* stolen, or was it a report on *stolen vehicles*?

Rule 6. When using numbers, hyphenate spans or estimates of time, distance, or other quantities. Remember not to use spaces around hyphens.

Examples:	*3:15-3:45 p.m.*
	1999-2016
	300-325 people

Rule 7. Hyphenate all compound numbers from *twenty-one* through *ninety-nine*.

Examples:	*thirty-two children*
	one thousand two hundred twenty-one dollars

Rule 8. Hyphenate all spelled-out fractions.

Example:	*more than two-thirds of registered voters*

Rule 9. Hyphenate most double last names.

> *Example*: *Sir Winthrop Heinz-Eakins will attend.*

Rule 10. As important as hyphens are to clear writing, they can become an annoyance if overused. Avoid adding hyphens when the meaning is clear. Many phrases are so familiar (e.g., *high school, twentieth century, one hundred percent*) that they can go before a noun without risk of confusing the reader.

> *Examples*: *a high school senior*
> *a twentieth century throwback*
> *one hundred percent correct*

Rule 11. When in doubt, look it up. Some familiar phrases may require hyphens. For instance, is a book *up to date* or *up-to-date*? Don't guess; have a dictionary close by, or look it up online.

Hyphens with Prefixes and Suffixes

A **prefix** (*a-, un-, de-, ab-, sub-, post-, anti-*, etc.) is a letter or set of letters placed before a **root** word. The word *prefix* itself contains the prefix *pre-*. Prefixes expand or change a word's meaning, sometimes radically: the prefixes *a-, un-*, and *dis-*, for example, change words into their opposites (e.g., *political*, **a**political; *friendly*, **un**friendly; *honor*, **dis**honor).

Rule 1. Hyphenate prefixes when they come before proper nouns or proper adjectives.

> *Examples*: *trans-American*
> *mid-July*

Rule 2. For clarity, many writers hyphenate prefixes ending in a vowel when the root word begins with the same letter.

> *Examples*: *ultra-ambitious*
> *semi-invalid*
> *re-elect*

Rule 3. Hyphenate all words beginning with the prefixes *self-, ex-* (i.e., *former*), and *all-*.

> *Examples*: *self-assured*
> *ex-mayor*
> *all-knowing*

Rule 4. Use a hyphen with the prefix *re-* when omitting the hyphen would cause confusion with another word.

> *Examples*:   *Will she recover from her illness?*
> *I have re-covered the sofa twice.*
> Omitting the hyphen would cause confusion with *recover*.
> *I must re-press the shirt.*
> Omitting the hyphen would cause confusion with *repress*.
> *The stamps have been reissued.*
> A hyphen after *re-* is not needed because there is no confusion with
>   another word.

Rule 5. Writers often hyphenate prefixes when they feel a word might be distracting or confusing without the hyphen.

> *Examples*:   *de-ice*
> With no hyphen we get *deice*, which might stump readers.
> *co-worker*
> With no hyphen we get *coworker*, which could be distracting
>   because it starts with *cow*.

A **suffix** (*-y, -er, -ism, -able*, etc.) is a letter or set of letters that follows a root word. Suffixes form new words or alter the original word to perform a different task. For example, the noun *scandal* can be made into the adjective *scandalous* by adding the suffix *-ous*. It becomes the verb *scandalize* by adding the suffix *-ize*.

Rule 1. Suffixes are not usually hyphenated. Some exceptions: *-style, -elect, -free, -based*.

> *Examples*:   *Modernist-style paintings*
> *Mayor-elect Smith*
> *sugar-free soda*
> *oil-based sludge*

Rule 2. For clarity, writers often hyphenate when the last letter in the root word is the same as the first letter in the suffix.

> *Examples*:   *graffiti-ism*
> *wiretap-proof*

Rule 3. Use discretion—and sometimes a dictionary—before deciding to place a hyphen before a suffix. But do not hesitate to hyphenate a rare usage if it avoids confusion.

Examples: *the annual dance-athon*

an eel-esque sea creature

Although the preceding hyphens help clarify unusual terms, they are optional and might not be every writer's choice. Still, many readers would scratch their heads for a moment over *danceathon* and *eelesque*.

DASHES

Dashes, like commas, semicolons, colons, ellipses, and parentheses, indicate added emphasis, an interruption, or an abrupt change of thought. Experienced writers know that these marks are not interchangeable. Note how dashes subtly change the tone of the following sentences:

Examples: *You are the friend, the only friend, who offered to help me.*

You are the friend—the only friend—who offered to help me.

I pay the bills; she has all the fun.

I pay the bills—she has all the fun.

I wish you would…oh, never mind.

I wish you would—oh, never mind.

Rule 1. Words and phrases between dashes are not generally part of the subject.

Example: *Joe—and his trusty mutt—**was** always welcome.*

Rule 2. Dashes replace otherwise mandatory punctuation, such as the commas after *Iowa* and *2013* in the following examples:

Without dash: *The man from Ames, Iowa, arrived.*
With dash: *The man—he was from Ames, Iowa—arrived.*
Without dash: *The May 1, 2013, edition of the* Ames Sentinel *arrived in June.*
With dash: *The* Ames Sentinel—*dated May 1, 2013—arrived in June.*

Rule 3. Some writers and publishers prefer spaces around dashes.

Example: *Joe — and his trusty mutt — was always welcome.*

ELLIPSES

Definition

- An **ellipsis** (plural: *ellipses*) is a punctuation mark consisting of three dots.

Use an ellipsis when omitting a word, phrase, line, paragraph, or more from a quoted passage. Ellipses save space or remove material that is less relevant. They are useful in getting right to the point without delay or distraction:

Full quotation: *"Today, after hours of careful thought, we vetoed the bill."*
With ellipsis: *"Today...we vetoed the bill."*

Although ellipses are used in many ways, the three-dot method is the simplest. Newspapers, magazines, and books of fiction and nonfiction use various approaches that they find suitable.

Some writers and editors feel that no spaces are necessary.

Example: *I don't know...I'm not sure.*

Others enclose the ellipsis with a space on each side.

Example: *I don't know ... I'm not sure.*

Still others put a space either directly before or directly after the ellipsis.

Examples: *I don't know ...I'm not sure.*
              I don't know... I'm not sure.

A four-dot method and an even more rigorous method used in legal works require fuller explanations that can be found in other reference books.

Rule 1. Many writers use an ellipsis whether the omission occurs at the beginning of a sentence, in the middle of a sentence, or between sentences.

A common way to delete the beginning of a sentence is to follow the opening quotation mark with an ellipsis, plus a bracketed capital letter:

Example: *"...[A]fter hours of careful thought, we vetoed the bill."*

Other writers omit the ellipsis in such cases, feeling the bracketed capital letter gets the point across.

For more on brackets, see "Parentheses and Brackets," earlier in this chapter.

Rule 2. Ellipses can express hesitation, changes of mood, suspense, or thoughts trailing off. Writers also use ellipses to indicate a pause or wavering in an otherwise straightforward sentence.

> **Examples**:   *I don't know…I'm not sure.*
> *Pride is one thing, but what happens if she…?*
> *He said, "I…really don't…understand this."*

QUESTION MARKS

Rule 1. Use a question mark only after a direct question.

> **Correct**:   *Will you go with me?*
> **Incorrect**:   *I'm asking if you will go with me?*

Rule 2a. A question mark replaces a period at the end of a sentence.

> **Incorrect**:   *Will you go with me?.*

Rule 2b. Because of Rule 2a, capitalize the word that follows a question mark. Some writers choose to overlook this rule in special cases.

> **Example**:   *Will you go with me? with Joe? with anyone?*

Rule 3a. Avoid the common trap of using question marks with **indirect questions**, which are statements that contain questions. Use a period after an indirect question.

> **Incorrect**:   *I wonder if he would go with me?*
> **Correct**:   *I wonder if he would go with me.*
> **OR**
> *I wonder: Would he go with me?*

Rule 3b. Some sentences are statements—or demands—in the form of a question. They are called **rhetorical questions** because they don't require or expect an answer. Many should be written without question marks.

> **Examples**:   *Why don't you take a break.*
> *Would you kids knock it off.*
> *What wouldn't I do for you!*

Rule 4. Use a question mark when a sentence is half statement and half question.

    Example: *You do care, don't you?*

Rule 5. The placement of question marks with quotation marks follows logic. If a question is within the quoted material, a question mark should be placed inside the quotation marks.

    Examples: *She asked, "Will you still be my friend?"*
                The question is part of the quotation.
                Do you agree with the saying, "All's fair in love and war"?
                The question is outside the quotation.

EXCLAMATION POINTS

Rule 1. Use an exclamation point to show emotion, emphasis, or surprise.

    Examples: *I'm truly shocked by your behavior!*
                Yay! We won!

Rule 2. An exclamation point replaces a period at the end of a sentence.

    Incorrect: *I'm truly shocked by your behavior!.*

Rule 3. Do not use an exclamation point in formal business writing.

Rule 4. Overuse of exclamation points is a sign of undisciplined writing. Do not use even one of these marks unless you're convinced it is justified.

CHAPTER 3

CAPITALIZATION

Capitalization is the writing of a word with its first letter in uppercase and the remaining letters in lowercase. Experienced writers are stingy with capitals. It is best not to use them if there is any doubt.

Rule 1. Capitalize the first word of a document and the first word after a period.

Rule 2. Capitalize proper nouns—and adjectives derived from proper nouns.

> *Examples*: *the Golden Gate Bridge*
> *the Grand Canyon*
> *a Russian song*
> *a Shakespearean sonnet*
> *a Freudian slip*

With the passage of time, some words originally derived from proper nouns have taken on a life, and authority, of their own and no longer require capitalization.

> *Examples*: *herculean* (from the ancient-Greek hero Hercules)
> *quixotic* (from the hero of the classic novel *Don Quixote*)
> *draconian* (from ancient-Athenian lawgiver Draco)

The main function of capitals is to focus attention on particular elements within any group of people, places, or things. We can speak of *a lake in the middle of the country*, or we can be more specific and say *Lake Michigan*, which distinguishes it from every other lake on earth.

Capitalization Reference List

- Brand names

- Companies

- Days of the week and months of the year

- Governmental matters
  Congress (but *congressional*), *the U.S. Constitution* (but *constitutional*), *the Electoral College, Department of Agriculture.* **Note:** Many authorities do not capitalize *federal* or *state* unless it is part of the official title: *State Water Resources Control Board,* but *state water board; Federal Communications Commission,* but *federal regulations.*

- Historical episodes and eras
  the Inquisition, the American Revolutionary War, the Great Depression

- Holidays

- Institutions
  Oxford College, the Juilliard School of Music

- Manmade structures
  the Empire State Building, the Eiffel Tower, the Titanic

- Manmade territories
  Berlin, Montana, Cook County

- Natural and manmade landmarks
  Mount Everest, the Hoover Dam

- Nicknames and epithets
  Andrew "Old Hickory" Jackson; Babe Ruth, the Sultan of Swat

- Organizations
  American Center for Law and Justice, Norwegian Ministry of the Environment

- Planets
  Mercury, Venus, Mars, Jupiter, Saturn, Uranus, Neptune, but policies vary on capitalizing *earth,* and it is usually not capitalized unless it is being discussed specifically as a planet: *We learned that Earth travels through space at 66,700 miles per hour.*

- Races, nationalities, and tribes
  Eskimo, Navajo, East Indian, Caucasian, African American (**Note:** *white* and *black* in reference to race are lowercase)

- Religions and names of deities
  Note: Capitalize *the Bible* (but *biblical*). Do not capitalize *heaven, hell, the devil, satanic.*

- Special occasions
  the Olympic Games, the Cannes Film Festival
- Streets and roads

Lowercase Reference List

Here is a list of categories *not* capitalized unless an item contains a proper noun or proper adjective (or, sometimes, a trademark). In such cases, only the proper noun or adjective is capitalized.

- Animals
  antelope, black bear, Bengal tiger, yellow-bellied sapsucker, German shepherd
- Elements
  Always lowercase, even when the name is derived from a proper noun: *einsteinium, nobelium, californium*
- Foods
  Lowercase except for brand names, proper nouns and adjectives, or custom-named recipes: *Tabasco sauce, Russian dressing, pepper crusted bluefin tuna, Mandy's Bluefin Surprise*
- Heavenly bodies besides planets
  Never capitalize the *moon* or the *sun*.
- Medical conditions
  Epstein-Barr syndrome, tuberculosis, Parkinson's disease
- Minerals
- Plants, vegetables, and fruits
  poinsettia, Douglas fir, Jerusalem artichoke, organic celery, Golden Delicious apples
- Seasons and seasonal data
  spring, summertime, the winter solstice, the autumnal equinox, daylight saving time

Rule 3. A thorny aspect of capitalization: where does it stop? When does the *Iraq war* become the *Iraq War*? Why is the legendary *Hope Diamond* not the *Hope diamond*? Everyone writes *New York City*, so why does the *Associated Press Stylebook* recommend *New York state*? There aren't always easy formulas or logical explanations. Research with reference books and search engines is the best strategy.

In the case of brand names, companies are of little help, because they capitalize any word that applies to their merchandise. *Domino's Pizza* or *Domino's pizza*? Is it *Ivory Soap* or *Ivory soap*, a *Hilton Hotel* or a *Hilton hotel*? Most writers don't capitalize common nouns that simply describe the products (*pizza, soap, hotel*), but it's not always easy to determine where a brand name ends. There is *Time* magazine but also the *New York Times Magazine*. No one would argue with *Coca-Cola* or *Pepsi Cola*, but a case could be made for *Royal Crown cola*.

If a trademark starts with a lowercase word or letter (e.g., *eBay*, *iPhone*), many authorities advise capitalizing it to begin a sentence.

Example: *EBay opened strong in trading today.*

Rule 4. Capitalize titles when they are used before names, unless the title is followed by a comma. Do not capitalize the title if it is used after a name or instead of a name.

Examples: *The president will address Congress.*
Chairman of the Board William Bly will preside at the conference.
The chairman of the board, William Bly, will preside.
The senators from Iowa and Ohio are expected to attend.
Also expected to attend are Senators Buzz James and Eddie Twain.
*The governors, lieutenant governors, and attorneys general called for a
    special task force.*
*Governor Fortinbrass, Lieutenant Governor Poppins, and Attorney General
    Dalloway will attend.*

NOTE

Out of respect, some writers and publishers choose to capitalize the highest
ranks in government, royalty, religion, etc.

Examples: *The President arrived.*
The Queen spoke.
The Pope decreed.

Many American writers believe this to be a wrongheaded policy in a country
where, theoretically, all humans are perceived as equal.

Rule 5. Titles are not the same as occupations. Do not capitalize occupations before full names.

Examples: *director Steven Spielberg*
owner Helen Smith
coach Biff Sykes

Sometimes the line between title and occupation gets blurred. One example is *general manager*: is it a title or an occupation? Opinions differ. Same with *professor*: the *Associated Press*

Stylebook considers *professor* a job description rather than a title, and recommends using lower-case even before the full name: *professor Robert Ames.*

Rule 6a. Capitalize a formal title when it is used as a direct address.

> **Example:**   *Will you take my temperature, Doctor?*

Rule 6b. Capitalize relatives' family names (kinship names) when they immediately precede a personal name, or when they are used alone in place of a personal name.

> **Examples:**   *I found out that Mom is here.*
> *You look good, Grandpa.*
> *Andy and Opie loved Aunt Bee's apple pies.*

However, these monikers are not capitalized with possessive nouns or pronouns, when they follow the personal name, or when they are not referencing a specific person.

> **Examples:**   *My mom is here.*
> *Joe's grandpa looks well.*
> *The James brothers were notorious robbers.*
> *There's not one mother I know who would allow that.*

Rule 6c. Capitalize nicknames in all cases.

> **Examples:**   *Meet my brothers, Junior and Scooter.*
> *I just met two guys named Junior and Scooter.*

Rule 7. Capitalize specific geographical regions. Do not capitalize points of the compass.

> **Examples:**   *We had three relatives visit from the West.*
> *Go west three blocks and then turn left.*
> *We left Florida and drove north.*
> *We live in the Southeast.*
> *We live in the southeast section of town.*
> *Most of the West Coast is rainy this time of year.* (referring to the United
>   States)
> *The west coast of Scotland is rainy this time of year.*

Some areas have come to be capitalized for their fame or notoriety:

> **Examples:**   *I'm from New York's Upper West Side.*
> *I'm from the South Side of Chicago.*
> *You live in Northern California; he lives in Southern California.*

Rule 8. In general, do not capitalize the word *the* before proper nouns.

Examples: *I'm reading the* London Times.
        They're fans of the Grateful Dead.

In special cases, if the word *the* is an inseparable part of something's official title, it may be capitalized.

Example: *We visited The Hague.*

Rule 9. Do not capitalize *city, town, county*, etc., if it comes before the proper name.

Examples: *the city of New York*
        New York City
        the county of Marin
        Marin County

Rule 10. Always capitalize the first word in a complete quotation, even midsentence.

Example: *Bill said, "That job we started last April is done."*

Rule 11. For emphasis, writers sometimes capitalize a midsentence independent clause or question.

Examples: *One of her cardinal rules was, Never betray a friend.*
        It made me wonder, What is mankind's destiny?

Rule 12. Capitalize the names of specific course titles, but not general academic subjects.

Examples: *I must take history and Algebra 101.*
        He has a double major in European economics and philosophy.

Rule 13. Capitalize art movements.

Example: *I like Surrealism, but I never understood Abstract Expressionism.*

Rule 14. Do not capitalize the first item in a list that follows a colon.

Example: *Bring the following: paper, a pencil, and a snack.*

For more on capitalization after a colon, go to "Colons," Rules 1, 3, and 4, in Chapter Two.

Rule 15. Do not capitalize "*the national anthem.*"

Rule 16a. Composition titles: which words should be capitalized in titles of books, plays, films, songs, poems, essays, chapters, etc.? This is a vexing matter, and policies vary. The usual advice is to capitalize only the "important" words. But this isn't really very helpful. Aren't all words in a title important?

The following rules for capitalizing composition titles are universal.

- Capitalize the title's first and last word.

- Capitalize verbs, including all forms of the verb *to be* (*is, are, was*, etc.).

- Capitalize all pronouns, including *it, he, who, that*, etc.

- Capitalize *not*.

- Do not capitalize *a, an*, or *the* unless it is first or last in the title.

- Do not capitalize the word *and, or*, or *nor* unless it is first or last in the title.

- Do not capitalize the word *to*, with or without an infinitive, unless it is first or last in the title.

Otherwise, styles, methods, and opinions vary. Small words such as *or, as, if*, and *but* are capped by some, but lowercased by others.

The major bone of contention is prepositions. The *Associated Press Stylebook* recommends capitalizing all prepositions of more than three letters (e.g., *With, About, Across*). Others advise lowercase until a preposition reaches five or more letters. Still others say not to capitalize any preposition, even big words like *regarding* or *underneath*.

Hyphenated words in a title also present problems. There are no set rules. Some writers, editors, and publishers choose not to capitalize words following hyphens unless they are proper nouns or proper adjectives (*Ex-Marine* but *Ex-husband*). Others capitalize any word that would otherwise be capped in titles (*Prize-Winning, Up-to-Date*).

Rule. 16b. Many books have subtitles. When including these, put a colon after the work's title and follow the same rules of composition capitalization for the subtitle.

> **Example:** *The King's English: A Guide to Modern Usage*

Note that *A* is capitalized because it is the first word of the subtitle.

Suppose you are reviewing a book whose title on the cover is in capital letters: *THE STUFF OF THOUGHT*. Beneath, in smaller capital letters, is the subtitle, LANGUAGE AS A WINDOW INTO HUMAN NATURE. All sides would agree that the main title should be written, *The Stuff of Thought*. But depending on which capitalization policy you choose, the subtitle might be any of the following:

*Language **As** a Window **Into** Human Nature*

*Language **as** a Window **Into** Human Nature*

*Language **As** a Window **into** Human Nature*

*Language **as** a Window **into** Human Nature*

Capitalizing composition titles is fraught with gray areas. Pick a policy and be consistent.

CHAPTER 4

WRITING NUMBERS

Except for a few basic rules, spelling out numbers vs. using figures (also called numerals) is largely a matter of writers' preference. Again, consistency is the key.

Policies and philosophies vary from medium to medium. The two most influential guide-books for publishers, editors, and writers, the *Associated Press Stylebook* and the *Chicago Manual of Style*, have different approaches. The first recommends spelling out the numbers one through nine and using figures thereafter; *Chicago* recommends spelling out the numbers one through ninety-nine and using figures thereafter.

This is a complex topic, with many exceptions, and there is no consistency we can rely on among blogs, books, newspapers, and magazines. This chapter will confine itself to rules that all media seem to agree on.

Rule 1. Spell out all numbers beginning a sentence.

Examples: *Twenty-three hundred sixty-one victims were hospitalized.*
Nineteen fifty-six was quite a year.

Note: The *Associated Press Stylebook* makes an exception for years.

Example: *1956 was quite a year.*

Rule 2a. Hyphenate all compound numbers from twenty-one through ninety-nine.

Examples: *Forty-three people were injured in the train wreck.*
Twenty-seven of them were hospitalized.

Rule 2b. Hyphenate all written-out fractions.

Examples: *We recovered about two-thirds of the stolen cash.*
One-half is slightly less than five-eighths.

Rule 3a. With figures of four or more digits, use commas. Count three spaces to the left to place the first comma. Continue placing commas after every three digits. *Important*: do not include decimal points when doing the counting.

Examples: *1,054 people*
$2,417,592.21

Rule 3b. It is not necessary to use a decimal point or a dollar sign when writing out sums of less than a dollar.

Not advised: *He had only $0.60.*
Better: *He had only sixty cents.*
OR
He had only 60 cents.

Rule 4a. For clarity, use *noon* and *midnight* rather than *12:00 PM* and *12:00 AM*.

NOTE

AM and *PM* are also written *A.M.* and *P.M.*, *a.m.* and *p.m.*, and *am* and *pm*. Some put a space between the time and *AM* or *PM*.

Examples: *8 AM*
3:09 P.M.
11:20 p.m.

Others write times using no space before *AM* or *PM*.

Examples: *8AM*
3:09P.M.
11:20p.m.

For the top of the hour, some write *9:00 PM*, whereas others drop the *:00* and write *9 PM* (or *9 p.m.*, *9PM*, etc.).

Rule 4b. Using numerals for the time of day has become widely accepted.

> *Examples*:   *The flight leaves at 6:22 a.m.*
> *Please arrive by 12:30 sharp.*

However, some writers prefer to spell out the time, particularly when using *o'clock*.

> *Examples*:   *She takes the four thirty-five train.*
> *The baby wakes up at five o'clock in the morning.*

Rule 5. Mixed fractions are often expressed in figures unless they begin a sentence.

> *Examples*:   *We expect a 5 ½ percent wage increase.*
> *Five and one-half percent was the expected wage increase.*

Rule 6. The simplest way to express large numbers is usually best.

> *Example*:   *twenty-three hundred* (simpler than *two thousand three hundred*)

Large round numbers are often spelled out, but be consistent within a sentence.

> *Consistent*:   *You can earn from one million to five million dollars.*
> *Inconsistent*:   *You can earn from one million dollars to 5 million dollars.*
> *Inconsistent*:   *You can earn from $1 million to five million dollars.*

Rule 7. Write decimals using figures. As a courtesy to readers, many writers put a zero in front of the decimal point.

> *Examples*:   *The plant grew 0.79 inches last year.*
> *The plant grew only 0.07 inches this year.*

Rule 8. When writing out a number of three or more digits, the word *and* is not necessary. However, use the word *and* to express any decimal points that may accompany these numbers.

> *Examples*:   *one thousand one hundred fifty-four dollars*
> *one thousand one hundred fifty-four dollars and sixty-one cents*
> *Simpler*:   *eleven hundred fifty-four dollars and sixty-one cents*

Rule 9. The following examples are typical when using figures to express dates.

> *Examples*:   *the 30th of June, 1934*
> *June 30, 1934* (no *-th* necessary)

Rule 10. When spelling out decades, do not capitalize them.

> *Example*:   *During the eighties and nineties, the U.S. economy grew.*

Rule 11. When expressing decades using figures, it is simpler to put an apostrophe before the incomplete numeral and no apostrophe between the number and the *s*.

> *Example*:   *During the '80s and '90s, the U.S. economy grew.*

Some writers place an apostrophe after the number:

Example: *During the 80's and 90's, the U.S. economy grew.*
Awkward: *During the '80's and '90's, the U.S. economy grew.*

Rule 12. You may also express decades in complete numerals. Again, it is cleaner to avoid an apostrophe between the year and the *s*.

> *Example*:   *During the 1980s and 1990s, the U.S. economy grew.*

CHAPTER 5

CONFUSING WORDS
AND HOMONYMS

Many words in English sound or look alike, causing confusion and not a few headaches. This chapter lists some of these words, and other troublemakers.

A

A, AN

Use *a* when the first letter of the word following has the sound of a consonant. Keep in mind that some vowels can sound like consonants, such as when they're sounded out as individual letters. Also, some letters, notably *h* and *u*, sometimes act as consonants (*home, usual*), other times as vowels (*honest, unusual*).

> *Examples*:   *a yearning*
> *a hotel*
> *a U-turn* (pronounced "yoo")
> *a NASA study*

Use *an* when the first letter of the word following has the sound of a vowel.

Examples: *an unfair charge*
                an honor (the *h* is silent)
                an HMO plan (*H* is pronounced "aitch")
                an NAACP convention (the *N* is pronounced "en")

ABBREVIATION, ACRONYM

This is a fine distinction that some consider nitpicking. Terms such as *FBI, HMO,* and *NAACP,* although widely called acronyms, are actually abbreviations. The difference is in how they are spoken. An *abbreviation,* also called an *initialism,* is pronounced letter by letter. An *acronym* is pronounced as if it were a word. The abbreviation *FBI* is pronounced "eff-bee-eye." The acronym *NASA* is pronounced "nassa."

ACCEPT, EXCEPT

Accept means "to acknowledge" or "to agree to."

Except is usually a preposition used to specify what isn't included: *I like all fruits except apples.*

ACRONYM

See **abbreviation, acronym**.

AD, ADD

Ad: short for "advertisement."

Add: to include; to perform addition.

ADAPT, ADOPT

To *adapt* is to take something and change it for a special purpose. A screenwriter adapts a book to make it work as a movie. An organism adapts (itself) to a new environment.

To *adopt* is to take something and use it or make it your own. A government adopts a different policy. A family adopts an orphan.

ADVERSE, AVERSE

Adverse: unfavorable: *an adverse reaction to the medication.*

Averse: not fond of; seeking to avoid: *averse to risk.*

ADVICE, ADVISE

Advice: guidance.

Advise: to suggest; to recommend.

AFFECT, EFFECT

Affect as a verb means "to influence": *It affected me strangely*. As a noun, it is a technical term used in psychology to describe someone's emotional state.

Effect as a noun means "result": *It had a strange effect on me*. As a verb, it means "to bring about" or "to cause": *He's trying to effect change in government*.

AGGRAVATE

This word is not a synonym for *annoy* or *irritate*. To *aggravate* is to make something worse: *He started running too soon and aggravated his sprained ankle*.

AHOLD

You can get *hold* of something, and you can get *a hold* of it. But in formal writing, "ahold" is not a real word.

AID, AIDE

An *aid* is a thing that helps.

An *aide* is a living helper or assistant: *His aide brought first aid*.

AIL, ALE

Ail: to be ill.

Ale: an alcoholic beverage.

AISLE, ISLE

Aisle: a corridor.

Isle: an island.

ALL READY, ALREADY

All ready means that everything or everyone is now ready.

Already refers to something accomplished earlier: *We already ate*.

ALL RIGHT

Two words. Someday, *alright* may finally prevail, but it hasn't yet.

ALL-TIME RECORD

The team set an all-time record for consecutive games won. Delete *all-time*. All records are "all-time" records.

Similarly, avoid "new record." The team set a record, not a new record.

ALL TOGETHER, ALTOGETHER

All together: in a group: *We're all together in this.*

Altogether: entirely: *It is not altogether his fault.*

ALLUDE, ELUDE, REFER

Allude means "to mention indirectly." Do not confuse *allude* with *refer*. If we say, "Good old Joe is here," we *refer* to Joe. If we say, "That man with the ready laugh is here," we *allude* to Joe, but we never mention his name.

Allude is also sometimes confused with *elude*, which means "to escape" or "avoid capture."

ALLUSION, ILLUSION

Allusion, the noun form of *allude*, is an indirect, sometimes sly, way of talking about something or someone.

An *illusion* is a false perception.

ALLOWED, ALOUD

Allowed: permitted.

Aloud: said out loud.

ALTAR, ALTER

Altar: a pedestal, usually religious.

Alter: to modify; to change.

AMBIGUOUS, AMBIVALENT

Something is *ambiguous* if it is unclear or has more than one meaning.

Ambivalent describes a mixed or undecided state of mind: *Her ambiguous remark left him feeling ambivalent about her.*

AMIABLE, AMICABLE

Both words mean "friendly," but *amiable* generally describes a pleasant person; *amicable* generally describes a cordial situation: *The amiable couple had an amicable divorce.*

AMID, AMIDST

Either is acceptable, but many writers prefer the more concise *amid*.

AMOUNT, NUMBER

Use *amount* for things that cannot be counted and *number* for things that can be counted: *This amount of water is enough to fill a number of bottles.*

The culprit is *amount*. Some might incorrectly say "a large amount of bottles," but no one would say "a large number of water."

a.m., p.m.

The abbreviation *a.m.* refers to the hours from midnight to noon, and *p.m.* refers to the hours from noon to midnight. Careful writers avoid such redundancies as *three a.m. in the morning* (delete *in the morning*) or *eight p.m. this evening* (make it *eight o'clock this evening*).

To avoid confusion, use *midnight* instead of *twelve a.m.* and *noon* instead of *twelve p.m.*

The terms also are frequently written as A.M., P.M.; AM, PM; and *am, pm*.

AN

See **a, an**.

AND/OR

"Objectionable to many, who regard it as a legalism," says Roy H. Copperud in *A Dictionary of Usage and Style*. Either say *and* or say *or*.

ANECDOTE, ANTIDOTE

An *anecdote* is a brief, amusing tale.

An *antidote* counteracts or reduces the effects of something unpleasant or even lethal. There are antidotes for snakebites, but there is no known antidote for boring anecdotes.

AN HISTORIC

Some speakers and writers use *an* with certain words starting with an audible *h*—the word *historic* heads the list. But why do those who say *an historic occasion* say *a hotel, a hospital, a happy home*? There is no valid reason to ever say *an historic, an heroic, an horrific*, etc., and anyone who does so is flirting with pomposity.

ANXIOUS, EAGER

In casual usage, *anxious* has become a synonym for *eager*, but the words are different. Whereas *eager* means "excited" or "enthusiastic," *anxious*, like *anxiety*, denotes uneasiness.

ANY MORE, ANYMORE

Use the two-word form to mean "any additional": *I don't need any more help.*
Use *anymore* to mean "any longer": *I don't need help anymore.*

ANY TIME, ANYTIME

Traditionalists do not accept the one-word form, *anytime*. But it is everywhere, and there's no turning back.

There does seem to be a difference between *You may call anytime* and *Do you have any time?* Always use the two-word form with a preposition: *You may call at any time.*

APPRAISE, APPRISE

A school district official was quoted as saying, "We have been appraised of all the relevant issues." Bad choice. The word *appraise* means "to decide the value of." The gentleman clearly meant *apprised*, which means "informed."

ASCENT, ASSENT

Ascent: a climb; movement upward.
Assent: an agreement (noun); to agree (verb).

AS REGARDS

See **in regard(s) to, with regard(s) to**.

ASSUME, PRESUME

Assume: to take for granted without evidence.
Presume: to believe based on evidence.

ASSURE, ENSURE, INSURE

To *assure* is to promise or say with confidence. It is more about saying than doing: *I assure you that you'll be warm enough.*

To *ensure* is to do or have what is necessary for success: *These blankets ensure that you'll be warm enough.*

To *insure* is to cover with an insurance policy.

What you *insure* you entrust to a business. What you *ensure* results from your personal efforts.

AURAL, ORAL

Since the two words are pronounced the same, be careful not to write *oral* (having to do with the mouth) if you mean *aural* (having to do with hearing).

AVERSE

See **adverse, averse**.

A WHILE, AWHILE

The two-word phrase *a while* is getting pushed aside by *awhile*. But *awhile* should only be used to mean "for a while." It's a distinction worth preserving: *It took a while, but I was convinced after thinking it over awhile.*

Always use *a while* with prepositions: *After a while, she arrived.*

B

BACKWARD, BACKWARDS

Both forms are acceptable, although the *Associated Press Stylebook* instructs journalists to always use *backward*.

BACTERIA

Staphylococcus is a virulent form of bacteria. No problem there. But in a sentence like *It's a virulent bacteria*, well, now we have a problem. *Bacteria* is a plural noun; the singular is *bacterium*. So don't write *The bacteria in the cut was infecting it*, because the bacteria *were* infecting it.

BAIL, BALE

Both words do double duty as noun and verb. As a noun, *bail* commonly refers to money deposited to gain a prisoner's freedom, or *bail* that prisoner *out*.

A *bale* is a large, bound or wrapped package of unprocessed material. To *bale* is to make into a bale.

BAITED BREATH, BATED BREATH

Don't write "baited breath." The word *bated*, a variant of *abated*, means "lessened in intensity," "restrained."

BALL, BAWL

Ball: a round object; a gala event.
Bawl: to cry; howl.

BARE, BEAR

Bare as an adjective means "unconcealed": *bare arms*. As a verb it means "expose": *to bare one's feelings*.

Bear as a noun refers to a wild animal. As a verb it has many meanings, from "carry" (*bear arms*) to "tolerate" (*I can't bear it*) to "steer" (*bear right at the corner*).

BASICALLY

This word, especially when it starts a sentence, is probably unnecessary.

BEACH, BEECH

The *beech* tree was close to the windy *beach*.

BEAT, BEET

You can't *beat* my recipe for *beets*.

BECAUSE, SINCE

Because and *since* can be used just about interchangeably to explain the reason for something. But *since* can also refer to a time in the past: *I have waited since yesterday.*

BELL, BELLE

Bell: a chime or alarm.
Belle: a lovely woman.

BENIGHTED

He was a benighted soul in an enlightened time. Many people associate it with *knighted* and think *benighted* is a good thing to be. Far from it. Note the lack of *a k*; don't think *knight*, think *night*. To be *benighted* is to be "in a state of moral or intellectual darkness."

BERTH, BIRTH

Berth: a built-in bed on a train or boat; a space for a boat to dock.
Birth: being born; a beginning.

BESIDE, BESIDES

Besides as an adverb means "in addition" or "moreover": *It's Albert's birthday, and besides, you promised. Besides* is also a preposition meaning "other than" or "except": *Who besides me is hungry?*

Compare that with *The person beside me is hungry. Beside* is a preposition that means "next to," "near," "alongside."

A lot of people say something is "besides the point." They mean *beside* the point. When a statement is beside the point, it misses the mark and settles nothing.

BETTER, BETTOR

Better: of higher quality.
Bettor: a gambler.

BIANNUAL, BIENNIAL, SEMIANNUAL

These words do not all mean the same thing. *Biannual* means "twice a year," as does *semiannual*, whereas *biennial* means "occurring every two years."

BITE, BYTE

Don't confuse what your teeth do with *byte*, a computer term for eight bits of information. Adding to the confusion, *sound bite*—a brief excerpt from a longer work—is sometimes mistakenly written "sound byte."

BLOC, BLOCK

The more familiar word is *block*, which can refer to many things: a toy, a cube-shaped object, a city street. Not as versatile is *bloc*: a group united for a particular purpose.

BOAR, BOOR, BORE

Boar: a wild pig.
Boor: a vulgar brute.
Bore: a compulsive chatterbox.

BOARD, BORED

When the *board* called the roll, he was too *bored* to speak up.

BOLDER, BOULDER

Bolder: more daring.

Boulder: a large rock.

BORN, BORNE

To be *born* is to be given birth to, as babies are born. Or it can mean "to be created": ideas are born the moment we think of them. It also means "to arise from": *Timmy's stomachache was born of wolfing his food.*

Borne is the past tense of *bear*, in the sense of "carry." To be *borne* is to be carried: *a mosquito-borne disease*; or to be endured: *Timmy's stomachache had to be borne until it finally went away.*

BOY, BUOY

Few if any would write *boy* instead of *buoy*, a nautical beacon or marker. Nonetheless, both words are traditionally pronounced the same. In *Bryson's Dictionary of Troublesome Words*, author Bill Bryson says, "Unless you would say 'boo-ee-ant' for *buoyant*, please return to pronouncing it 'boy.' "

BRAKE, BREAK

Use your *brake* before you *break* something.

BRIDAL, BRIDLE

Bridal: relating to brides and weddings.

A *bridle* is a head harness, usually for a horse. Not surprisingly, the verb *bridle* means "to control" or "to restrain." But it also means "to pull back the head quickly in anger."

BRING, TAKE

They're not interchangeable. You *bring* something here; you *take* something there. The locations of "here" and "there" are from the perspective of the speaker or writer. Your friend asks you to *bring* her a book, so you *take* the book to her home.

BROACH, BROOCH

To *broach* a topic is to bring it up for discussion: *Now is the time to broach the subject.* As a verb, *broach* also means "to open or enlarge a hole." The noun *broach* refers to a pointed tool which performs that operation.

A *brooch*, a decorative pin or clip, is nothing like a *broach*. But since they're often pronounced alike, and because ignorance never rests, some dictionaries accept *broach* as an alternative spelling of *brooch*.

BUOY

See **boy, buoy**.

BYTE

See **bite, byte**.

C

CACHE, CASH

As a noun, *cache* refers to a hidden supply of valuables, such as food, jewels, and *cash*. But it can also refer to the hiding place where you keep those items. The verb *cache* means "to hide treasure in a secret place": *He cached all his cash in a cache.*

CAN, MAY

I can go means I have the ability and freedom to go.
I may go means I have either an option or permission to go.

CANNON, CANON

Cannon: a large, mounted gun.
Canon: a body of writings; a principle or set of principles.

CANNOT

One word; avoid "can not."

CANVAS, CANVASS

Canvas is a durable fabric.
Canvass as a noun or a verb refers to the door-to-door gathering of votes or opinions.

CAPITAL, CAPITOL

Just remember: the *o* means it's a building. A *capitol* is a government building where a state legislature meets, and the *Capitol* is the building where the U.S. Congress meets.

A *capital* is a city that serves as the seat of government. *We got a tour of the capitol when we went to the capital.*

CARAT, CARET, KARAT

Most of the confusion is caused by *carat* and *karat* because both are associated with jewelry. The purity of gold is measured in *karats. Twenty-four-karat gold is 99.9 percent pure, but so soft that it is considered impractical for most jewelry.*

A *carat* is a weight measurement for gemstones: *a two-carat diamond set in an eighteen-karat gold ring.*

A *caret* has nothing to do with any of this. It is a mark an editor makes in a document to show where additional material should be inserted.

CAREEN, CAREER

Grammar sticklers are a stubborn lot. They use *career* the way everyone else uses *careen.* It is *career*, not *careen*, that means "to veer out of control": *The car careered wildly across three lanes. Careen* means "to lean or tip over," and strictly speaking, it's more suitable for describing boats than cars.

CAST, CASTE

Cast: a group of actors or individuals.

Caste: a social class; a rigid system of social distinctions.

CEMENT, CONCRETE

People constantly refer to "cement" sidewalks, driveways, walls, etc. However, *cement* is a powder that, when mixed with sand or gravel and water, becomes *concrete.*

CENSOR, CENSURE

They sound similar, and both words deal with negative criticism. *Censor* as a verb means "to remove unacceptable material." As a noun, it means "someone who censors."

Censure as a verb means "to disapprove of" or "to criticize strongly." As a noun, it means "disapproval," even "scorn."

CENTER AROUND

The lecture will center around the economy. The center is the middle point. Would you say "point around"? This common, muddleheaded expression results from scrambling *center on* and *revolve around*. Because those idioms are roughly synonymous, if you use them both enough, they merge in the mind.

CEREAL, SERIAL

Cereal: a breakfast food.

Serial: a story told in regular installments (noun); ongoing, in a series (adjectives).

CHAISE LOUNGE

This example of cultural dyslexia should be avoided at all costs. The correct term is *chaise longue*, meaning "long chair" in French.

CHILDISH, CHILDLIKE

Both are comparisons with children. The difference is that *childish* is unflattering; it's equivalent to *infantile* and only a small improvement on *babyish*. Someone is childish when acting unreasonable or bratty.

Not so with *childlike*, a word that extols youthful virtues, such as sweetness, purity, and innocence.

CHILE, CHILI

If life were fair, *Chile* with an *e* would refer only to a country in South America, and *chili* with a second *i* would refer to a type of pepper, and also to a spicy stew. These spellings are recommended, but with the caveat that not everyone agrees. In New Mexico, the stew they eat is *chile*, not *chili*. The stylebook of the *Los Angeles Times* says the dish is *chili*, but the pepper is a *chile*. And there are even some who spell the pepper or the dish *chilli*.

CHOMPING AT THE BIT

It started out as *champing at the bit*, which is still preferred by most dictionaries.

CHORAL, CORAL

Choral: relating to or sung by a choir.

Coral: an underwater organism that makes up reefs; a shade of orange.

CHORALE, CORRAL

A *chorale* can be both a piece of music and a singing group.

A *corral* is an enclosure for horses or other livestock.

CHORD, CORD

When two or more musical tones are sounded simultaneously, the result is a *chord*.
A *cord* is a rope or strand of flexible material.

CITE, SIGHT, SITE

Cite: to quote; to praise; to mention; to order to appear in court.
Sight: the ability to see; a scene or view.
Site: a location or position.

CLASSIC, CLASSICAL

Classic, adjective or noun, is a term of high praise: "of the finest quality" or "a prime example of": *a classic play, a classic pizza*.

The adjective *classical* applies to traditions going back to the ancient Greeks and Romans: *The house featured an array of classical influences.*

Classical music is marked by formal, sophisticated, extended compositions.

CLICHÉ

It's a noun, not an adjective. Yet more and more you see or hear things like *I know it sounds cliché, but…* Make it *I know it sounds **like a** cliché*.

CLICK, CLIQUE

A *click* is a brief percussive noise, but some mistakenly write it when they mean *clique*, a close, exclusive group of people.

CLIMACTIC, CLIMATIC

Climactic—note that middle *c*—means "exciting" or "decisive." It is often confused with *climatic*, which means "resulting from or influenced by climate."

CLOSE PROXIMITY

This phrase is a pompous and redundant way of saying "near." *Proximity* does not mean "distance"; it means "nearness," so *close proximity* means "close nearness."

COARSE, COURSE

Coarse means "rough, lacking in fineness of texture" or "crude, lacking in sensitivity."

Course is usually a noun and has several meanings, mostly having to do with movement or progress, whether it be a *course* taken in school or the *course* of a river.

COHORT

Your friend is a crony, confidant, or collaborator, but not a cohort. In ancient Rome, a *cohort* was a division of three hundred to six hundred soldiers. So careful speakers and writers avoid *cohort* when referring to one person. Your *cohort* is not your comrade, ally, teammate, or assistant. It's a whole group, gang, team, posse: *A cohort of laborers went on strike.*

COIN A PHRASE

To *coin a phrase* is to make one up. But many misuse it when citing or quoting familiar expressions: *His bright idea was, to coin a phrase, dead on arrival.* Since *dead on arrival* is a well-known idiom, the writer didn't "coin" it; he merely repeated it.

COINCIDENCE

See **irony**.

COLLECTABLE, COLLECTIBLE

Both are acceptable, but *collectible* has a slight edge in popularity, especially as a noun.

COLLIDE, CRASH

A *collision* involves two moving objects. A car does not *collide* with a lamppost; it *crashes* into a lamppost.

COMPLEMENT, COMPLIMENT

As both noun and verb, *complement* refers to an added element that enhances, rounds out, or puts a final touch on something.

Compliment, noun and verb, is about nice words or gestures. *Try this perfect complement to your order, with our compliments.*

COMPLETE, COMPLETELY

These words are often unnecessary. What is the difference between *a complete meltdown* and *a meltdown*? How is *completely exhausted* different from *exhausted*?

COMPRISE

Possibly the most abused two-syllable word in English. It means "contain," "consist of," "be composed of." Most problems could be avoided by remembering this mantra: *The whole comprises its parts.*

Consider this misuse: *Vegetables comprise 80 percent of my diet*. The correct sentence is *Eighty percent of my diet comprises vegetables*. My diet *consists of* vegetables; vegetables do not consist of my diet.

This sentence looks right to most people: *Joe, John, and Bob comprise the committee*. But it's the other way around: *The committee comprises Joe, John, and Bob*.

Another common misuse is the phrase *comprised of*, which is never correct. Most people use *comprised of* as an elegant-seeming alternative to *composed of*. An ad for a cleaning service states, "Our team is comprised of skilled housekeepers." Make it "Our team comprises skilled housekeepers," "Our team is composed of skilled housekeepers," or, perhaps the best choice, "Our team consists of skilled housekeepers."

Since *comprise* already means "composed of," anyone using *comprised of* is actually saying "composed of of."

CONCERTED

One person cannot make a *concerted* effort. A concert implies an orchestra. As Paul Brians points out in his *Common Errors in English Usage*, "To work 'in concert' is to work together with others. One can, however, make a *concentrated* effort."

CONCRETE

See **cement, concrete**.

CONFIDANT, CONFIDENT

Confidant: a trusted adviser.
Confident: certain, self-assured.

CONNIVE, CONSPIRE

One who *connives* pretends not to know while others are collaborating on something sneaky, wrong, or illegal.

To *conspire* is to work together on a secret scheme.

CONNOTE, DENOTE

Denote is used for descriptions that stick to the facts. The word "dog" *denotes* a domesticated animal.

Connote reveals additional meanings beyond what is clinical or objective. It is used when expressing what a word implies or reminds us of. The word "dog" *connotes* loyalty.

CONTINUAL, CONTINUOUS

The difference between *continual* and *continuous* is the subtle difference between *regular* and *nonstop*. If your car *continually* breaks down, it also runs some of the time.

A faucet that drips *continuously* never stops dripping, twenty-four hours a day. If a faucet drips *continually*, there are interludes when it's not dripping.

CONVINCE, PERSUADE

To many, these two are synonyms, but there are shades of difference. Someone might be persuaded, while at the same time, not convinced: *She persuaded me to do it, but I'm still not convinced it was right.* When something or someone *persuades* us to act, it might be by using reason or logic, but it could also be by using force, lies, or guilt.

Convince refers to an unforced change of mind and heart that precedes action. We consider the evidence, and if it is strong enough, it *convinces* us and changes our perspective.

In formal writing, *convince* never takes an infinitive, but *persuade* almost always does. You cannot be convinced *to do* something; you can only be convinced *that* something, or be convinced *of* something.

CORAL

See **choral, coral**.

CORD

See **chord, cord**.

CORRAL

See **chorale, corral**.

COUNCIL, COUNSEL

Council: a group of people meeting for a purpose.
Counsel: advice (noun); an attorney (noun); to give advice or guidance (verb).

COUPLE (OF)

The *of* stays. These days, even veteran communicators are saying and writing "couple miles from here" or "costs a couple bucks." That used to be the jargon of tough guys in gangster movies.

COURSE

See **coarse, course**.

CRASH

See **collide, crash**.

CRAVEN

To many people, a *craven scoundrel* is a flagrant or shameless rogue, not a spineless one. But *craven* means "cowardly," "weak."

CRITERIA

Criteria is the plural of *criterion*, a standard used for judging, deciding, or acting. The sentence *Honesty is our chief criteria* is ungrammatical; there can't be only one *criteria*. Make it *Honesty is our chief criterion* or *Honesty is one of our chief criteria*. Your criteria *are* your standards, plural.

Those who know that *criteria* is plural aren't out of the woods yet either: many believe the singular is "criterium." And there are some who will reveal to you their "criterias."

CURRENTLY

Often unnecessary. What is the difference between *I'm currently writing a book* and *I'm writing a book*?

D

DAILY BASIS

I run five miles on a daily basis. In most cases, the windy and unwieldy *on a daily basis* can be replaced with *daily* or *every day*.

DATA

John B. Bremner, in *Words on Words*, states unequivocally, "The word is plural." This one is thorny, because the singular, *datum*, is virtually nonexistent in English. Many people see *data* as a synonym for "information," and to them, *These data are very interesting* sounds downright bizarre. Maybe, but it's also correct. Theodore M. Bernstein, in *The Careful Writer*, says, "Some respected and learned writers have used *data* as a singular. But a great many more have not."

DEFINITE, DEFINITIVE

Something *definite* is exact, clearly defined, with no ambiguity. But *definite* does not necessarily mean "correct": *George has a definite belief that two and two are five.*

Something *definitive* is authoritative, the best, the last word: *This is the definitive biography of Lincoln.*

DENOTE

See **connote, denote**.

DESERT, DESSERT

The noun *desert* refers to a desolate area. As a verb, it means "to abandon."

A *dessert* is the final course of a meal.

Many misspell the phrase *just deserts*, meaning "proper punishment." In that usage, *deserts* is derived from *deserve*.

DESPISE

"Syme despised him and slightly disliked him," wrote George Orwell in the novel *1984*. Orwell knew that, strictly speaking, *despise* means "to look down on" but not necessarily "to dislike," although that's usually part of the deal.

DEVICE, DEVISE

Device: an invention.

Devise: to invent.

DIFFERENT FROM, DIFFERENT THAN

Different from is the standard phrase. Traditionalists obstinately avoid *different than*, especially in simple comparisons, such as *You are different from me.*

More-liberal linguists point out that a sentence like *It is no different for men than it is for women* is clear and concise, and rewriting it with *different from* could result in a clumsy clunker like *It is no different for men from the way it is for women.*

They may have a point, but many fine writers have had no problem steering clear of *different than* for their entire careers.

DILEMMA

Be careful when using *dilemma* as a synonym for *predicament*. The *di-* in *dilemma* (like that in *dichotomy* or *dioxide*) indicates *two*: if you have a dilemma, it means you're facing two tough choices.

DISBURSE, DISPERSE

To *disburse* is to distribute or pay out money or other financial assets.

Use *disperse* when something other than money is being distributed: *The agency dispersed pamphlets after the meeting.*

Disperse also means "to scatter" or "make disappear": *The police dispersed the unruly mob.*

DISCOMFIT, DISCOMFORT

The two are often confused. *Discomfit* originally meant "to defeat utterly." It has come to mean "to fluster," "to embarrass."

Discomfort is usually used as a noun meaning "anxiety," "nervousness."

DISCREET, DISCRETE

Discreet: careful not to attract attention, tactful.

Discrete: separate, detached.

People often write *discrete* when they mean *discreet*. The situation is not helped by *discretion*, the noun form of *discreet*.

DISINTERESTED, UNINTERESTED

You can be both uninterested and disinterested, or one but not the other. *Disinterested* means "impartial"; *uninterested* means "unconcerned" or "apathetic."

Many would interpret *The judge was disinterested* to mean that the judge didn't care. But the sentence actually means that the judge was unbiased. Huge difference there. Would you rather have a judge who's fair or one who wants to go home?

DOCK

What is often thought of as a *dock* is actually a *pier* or *wharf*. The book *Modern American Usage* (edited by Jacques Barzun, et al.) defines a *dock* as "the water-filled space in which the ship comes to rest. The *pier* is the structure on which the passengers stand or alight." Would Otis Redding's song still be a masterpiece if he'd called it *Sittin' on the Pier of the Bay*?

DRUG (DRAGGED)

She drug Joe out of his office at midnight. When did "drug" replace *dragged* as the past tense of *drag*? The answer is: It didn't, and it couldn't, and it better not.

DUAL, DUEL

Dual: double; having two parts.

Duel: a two-sided conflict (noun); to fight a duel (verb).

E

EAGER

See **anxious, eager**.

EFFECT

See **affect, effect**.

e.g., i.e.

These two helpful abbreviations are often used interchangeably, a sorry mistake that impoverishes the language. The term *i.e.* means "that is to say" or "in other words," whereas *e.g.* means "for example."

To illustrate: *Artists like Marlon Brando and James Dean (i.e., the so-called "method actors") electrified audiences in the 1950s.* Compare that sentence with *The so-called "method actors" (e.g., Marlon Brando and James Dean) electrified audiences in the 1950s.*

EKE OUT

It has come to mean "barely get by": *I eke out a living as a writer.* But its traditional meaning is either "to supplement": *I eke out my living as a writer by working a day job*, or "to make the most of": *We eked out the small amount of food we had left.*

ELUDE

See **allude, elude, refer**.

EMIGRATE, IMMIGRATE

Emigrate: to leave one country in order to live in another country. *Emigrate* takes the preposition *from*, as in *He emigrated from Russia to America.* It is incorrect to say. "He emigrated to America."

Immigrate: to enter a new country with the intention of living there. *Immigrate* takes the preposition *to*, as in *He immigrated to America from Russia.* It is incorrect to say, "He immigrated from Russia."

EMINENT, IMMINENT

Eminent: prominent; distinguished: *an eminent scholar.*
Imminent: about to happen: *in imminent danger.*

EMPATHY, SYMPATHY

When we have *empathy*, we are able to put ourselves in other people's place and even feel their pain, or think we do.

Sympathy is more removed than *empathy*. When we have *sympathy*, we may not suffer along with those who are hurting, but we have compassion and are often willing to help.

EMULATE, IMITATE

Emulate means "to try to be as good or successful as."

Imitate means "to copy or fashion oneself after."

A sentence like *He tried to emulate her* is repeating itself: He *tried to try* to be as good as she was. We don't "try to emulate." When we *emulate*, we're already trying.

ENORMITY

This word is frequently misused: the "enormity" of football linemen these days, or the "enormity" of the task. *Enormity* has nothing to do with something's size. For that, we have such words as *immensity, vastness, hugeness,* and *enormousness.*

Enormity is an ethical, judgmental word meaning "great wickedness," "a monstrous crime." *The enormity of Jonestown* doesn't mean Jonestown was a huge place, but rather that it was the site of a hugely outrageous tragedy.

ENSURE

See **assure, ensure, insure**.

ENTHUSE

Many writers, editors, scholars, and critics regard *enthuse* and *enthused* as unserious and unacceptable.

EPITAPH, EPITHET

An *epitaph* is a tribute inscribed on a tombstone in honor of the person buried there.

An *epithet*, unlike an epitaph, is often an insult based on race, class, religion, politics, etc.: *The mob was shouting racial epithets.*

Otherwise, an epithet is a kind of nickname. It is a word or brief phrase that illustrates a defining trait of someone or something: *Alexander the Great, the wine-dark sea.*

EPITOME

The epitome of means "the essence of." It does not mean "the best," "the height of." *Sam is the epitome of humility* means that Sam is a perfect example of a humble person. It doesn't necessarily mean that he's one of the humblest men who ever lived.

ERSTWHILE

It's often confused with *worthwhile*. But *erstwhile* means "previous" or "one-time." *My erstwhile assistant* does not mean "my valuable assistant." It means "my former assistant" and nothing more.

etc., et al.

These abbreviations are a scholarly way of saying, "You get the point."

The term *etc.* means "and the rest," "and so on." It is usually placed at the end of a short list of things to save the writer (and reader) the trouble of going on needlessly.

When a list of people, rather than things, is involved, use *et al.* in place of *etc.*: *Joe Smith, Ray Jones, et al., led the team to victory.*

Both *etc.* and *et al.* require periods, even midsentence.

EVERY DAY, EVERYDAY

The two-word term *every day* is an adverbial phrase that answers the questions *when* or *how often*, as in *I learn something new every day.*

As one word, *everyday* is an adjective that means "ordinary" or "part of a daily routine": *These are my everyday clothes.*

EXACERBATE, EXAGGERATE

To *exacerbate* is to make a difficult situation worse or more intense: *The humidity exacerbated the intense heat.*

To *exaggerate* (note the double g) is to overstate, to stretch the truth: *He exaggerated when he said it was the hottest day on record.*

EXCEPT

See **accept, except**.

F

FACTIOUS, FRACTIOUS

Factious means "characterized by dissent and internal disputes." A factious group is liable to split off into *factions*.

Fractious means "irritable," "quarrelsome," "ill-tempered."

FAINT, FEINT

Faint: to go unconscious.

Feint: a distracting move meant to throw an opponent off guard (from *feign*).

FAIR, FARE

Fair: an exhibition (noun); just, impartial (adjectives).

Fare: payment for travel (noun); to have an experience (verb); to go through something (verb): *How did you fare on your test?*

FARTHER, FURTHER

The general rule: *farther* refers to real, physical distance: *Let's walk a little farther.*

Further deals with degree or extent: *Let's discuss this further.*

FAZE, PHASE

When something or someone *fazes* you, you are disturbed or troubled: *Her behavior doesn't faze me.*

A *phase* is a period or chapter: *He's going through a difficult phase right now.*

FEAT, FEET

Feat: an extraordinary act or accomplishment.

Feet: twelve-inch increments; appendages below the ankles.

FEWER, LESS

Here's a seemingly innocent sentence: *I now have two less reasons for going.* Make it *two fewer reasons.* If you can count the commodity (two reasons), *less* will be wrong. You have *less justification*, but *fewer reasons.*

Exception: When the amount is *one*, such a sentence should read, "I now have *one* reason *fewer*" or "*one less* reason, but not "*one fewer* reason." Admittedly, this is a head-scratcher, but that's English for you.

Use *less* for specific measurements of money, distance, time, or weight: *It costs less than a million dollars. We walked less than fifty feet. Less than thirty minutes had passed. It weighs less than five pounds.* The book *Modern American Usage* explains why: "We take a *million dollars* as a sum of money, not as a number of units; *fifty feet* as a measure of distance, not as one foot added to forty-nine other feet; *thirty minutes* as a stretch of time, exactly like half an hour…and the quantitative *less* is therefore correct in comparisons; *fewer* would sound absurd."

FIR, FUR

Fir: a type of tree.
Fur: animal hair.

FIRSTLY

See **secondly, thirdly, fourthly**.

FLAIR, FLARE

Flair: style; talent.
Flare: to erupt; to blaze.

FLAMMABLE, INFLAMMABLE

Let's see: *flammable* means "combustible." *Inflammable* means "combustible." Any questions?

FLAUNT, FLOUT

He was a rebel who flaunted the rules. That sentence is incorrect. Make it *flouted the rules.* To *flout* is to ignore, disregard, defy.

To *flaunt* is to make a big display: *She flaunted her diamond necklace.*

FLEA, FLEE

Flea: a type of insect.
Flee: to run away.

FLOUNDER, FOUNDER

One way to avoid confusing these two verbs is to think of *flounder*, the fish. Something that is *floundering* is thrashing around helplessly, like a fish out of water.

Founder means "to fail." If a business is *floundering*, it is in distress but may yet be saved. If a business *founders*, nothing can revive it.

FLOUR, FLOWER

Flour: an edible powder prepared by grinding grains.
Flower: the bloom of a plant.

FOREGO, FORGO

Many permissive editors allow *forego* in place of *forgo*. But *forego* means "to go before," "precede": *A good stretching session should forego rigorous exercise.*

To *forgo* is to abstain from, do without: *If you forgo a good stretching session, you might pull a muscle.*

FOREWORD, FORWARD

A *foreword* is an introduction, usually to a book. It's sometimes confused with *forward*, meaning "ahead," "forth."

FORMER

See **latter**.

FORTH, FOURTH

Forth: onward.
Fourth: coming directly after whatever is third.

FORTUITOUS, FORTUNATE

Fortuitous is a chronically misunderstood word. To purists, it most emphatically does not mean "lucky" or "fortunate"; it simply means "by chance." You are *fortunate* if you win the lottery *fortuitously*, but you can also get flattened by a truck *fortuitously*.

FOUL, FOWL

Foul: tainted; sickening.
Fowl: edible bird or birds.

FRACTIOUS

See **factious, fractious**.

FREE GIFT

A curious term for *gift*.

FULSOME

Many people take *fulsome* to mean "abundant" or "lavish." But be wary of writing the likes of *He received a fulsome tribute* or *Please accept my fulsome apology.* The word actually means something darker: "excessive," "fawning," even "disgusting."

FUN

Fun is a noun, not an adjective. Sentences like *It was a fun time* or the ghastly *It was so fun* have no place in serious writing.

FUR

See **fir, fur**.

FURTHER

See **farther, further**.

G

GAIT, GATE

Gait: stride; the way a person or animal walks or runs.
Gate: a barrier.

GAMUT

Gamut originally referred to the entire range of musical notes that the ear can recognize. It has come to mean the range or extent of anything: *His speech ran a gamut of emotions*. Do not confuse *run the gamut* with *run the gantlet* (see **gantlet, gauntlet**).

GANTLET, GAUNTLET

These two words, despite their similarity, come from different roots. The distinction should be preserved.

The expression *run the gantlet* means "to undergo criticism or harassment from several sources in a concentrated period of time." It is often written *run the gauntlet*, which makes language nitpickers cry foul.

To *throw down the gauntlet* is to aggressively challenge someone. To *take up the gauntlet* is to accept such a challenge.

GEL, JELL

In popular usage, *jell* means "to come together": *Our team is starting to jell*. *Gel* refers to a jellylike substance: *hair gel*.

GILT, GUILT

Gilt: gold coating.
Guilt: fault; blame; shame.

GLIB

A word with a split personality suitable for backhanded compliments and faint praise. *Glib* can mean "smooth," "urbane." But it can also mean "superficial," "too slick."

GRADUATE

He graduated high school last weekend. Make it *graduated from.* There are even some fuss-budgets who'd insist he *was graduated from* high school. But *graduated from* is as correct as *was graduated from.*

GRAFFITI

Note the double *f* and single *t. Graffiti* is the plural of *graffito,* Italian for "little scratching." Therefore, *There was graffiti all over the wall* is incorrect. Make it *There **were** graffiti all over the wall.*

GRILL, GRILLE

Grill: a grated metal cooking utensil (noun); to cook over direct heat (verb).
Grille: a network of metal, wooden, or plastic bars that acts as a barrier or screen.

GRISLY, GRISTLY, GRIZZLY

Grisly means "horrific," "gruesome." However, grisly bears are not necessarily *grizzly bears,* North American brown bears known for their fierceness.
Don't confuse *grisly* with *gristly,* which means "tough," "chewy."

GUERRILLA

Note the spelling: double *r,* double *l.* Some think "guerilla" with one *r* is a valid alternative, but the word derives from *guerra,* which means "war" in Spanish.

H

HAIR, HARE

Hair: what grows on the head and body.
Hare: a rabbit.

HALL, HAUL

Hall: a passageway; a large room.
Haul: to pull or drag.

HALVE, HAVE

Halve: to divide in two.
Have: to possess; to hold.

HANGAR, HANGER

Many think that a shed or shelter for housing airplanes is a "hanger," rather than a *hangar* (the correct spelling).

A *hanger* is something to hang a garment on, or someone who hangs things.

HANGED, HUNG

Speakers and writers who value precision know that the past tense of *hang*, when it means "to put to death using a rope," is *hanged*, not *hung*. This applies to both the active and passive voice: *They hanged the prisoner* and *The prisoner was hanged*.

For inanimate objects, use *hung*. Under unusual conditions, people also *hung* or *are hung*, e.g., *He hung from the tree with one hand* or *He found himself hung upside down*.

HEAL, HEEL

Heal: to repair; to restore to health.
Heel: the back part of the foot; a scoundrel.

HEALTHFUL, HEALTHY

The difference between these two words is unquestionable, *healthful* meaning "something that promotes health" and *healthy* meaning "in good health." But in everyday speech, *healthful* has been nudged aside by *healthy* in phrases like *healthy food* or *a healthy diet*.

HEAR, HERE

There is an *ear* in *hear*, and *here* is 80 percent of *where*.

HEROIN, HEROINE

Heroin: a drug derived from morphine.
Heroine: a woman admired for courage or ability.

HISTORIC

See **an historic**.

HOARD, HORDE

Hoard: to stockpile; to amass.
Horde: a large group; a crowd.

HOARSE, HORSE

Hoarse: raspy; sore-throated.

Horse: a type of animal.

HOLE, WHOLE

Hole: an opening.

Whole: entirety (noun); entire (adjective).

HOLY, WHOLLY

Holy: sacred.

Wholly: entirely.

HOMAGE

A critic called a film "a homage to motherhood." The critic wisely did not write "an homage," knowing full well that the *h* is sounded (see **an historic**). This word has spun out of control in the twenty-first century. Its traditional pronunciation is "HOMM-ij." Then "AHM-ij" gained a foothold, and it went downhill from there. Now, just about all one hears is the pseudo-sophisticated "oh-MAHZH," a pronunciation that was virtually nonexistent in English until the late twentieth century.

HONE IN

Make it *home in*. *Hone in* has achieved undeserved legitimacy for the worst of reasons: the similarity in sound and appearance of *n* and *m*. *Honing* is a technique used for sharpening cutting tools and the like.

To *home in*, like *zero in*, is to get something firmly in your sights, to get to the crux of a problem.

HOT WATER HEATER

A curious term for *water heater*.

HUNG

See **hanged, hung**.

I

IDLE, IDOL, IDYLL

Idle: not active; unemployed.

Idol: an effigy; a beloved celebrity.

Idyll: a happy interlude; prose or poetry describing rural serenity.

i.e.

See **e.g., i.e.**

ILLUSION

See **allusion, illusion**.

IMITATE

See **emulate, imitate**.

IMMIGRATE

See **emigrate, immigrate**.

IMMINENT

See **eminent, imminent**.

IMPACT

As a verb, *impact* is constantly misused, and *affect* is almost always the better choice. Avoid such usages as *The proposition will impact property taxes* or *Greenhouse gas emissions negatively impact the environment*. Make it *affect* instead of *impact* in both sentences.

Impact means "to pack tightly together," as in *an impacted tooth*.

IMPLY, INFER

Infer is not a synonym for *imply*. *Imply* is done by a speaker or writer—specifically, one who is being indirect: *She implied that I'm a fool* means that she didn't come right out and say it, but she got her point across.

Infer is done by a perceptive listener or reader who "catches" your meaning: *I infer that you think I'm a fool*.

Imply is akin to *suggest* and *insinuate; infer* is akin to *deduce* and *conclude*.

INCITE, INSIGHT

Incite: to provoke; stir up.

Insight: understanding; comprehension.

INCLUDE

From a story about a rescue at sea: "The rescued pair included an American woman and a Danish man." This is a misuse of *include*, which means "to make someone or something part of a group." You can't be *included* unless others are involved. The sentence requires a rewrite, something like *The two people rescued were an American woman and a Danish man.*

A major-league baseball team doesn't *include* men; it *consists of* men, and only men. Compare: *Our office softball team includes women.* We realize immediately that it's a coed league and there are also men on the squad.

INCREDIBLE, INCREDULOUS

Something *incredible* is beyond belief, so when we experience it, we are *incredulous.*

Incredulous refers to a state of astonishment or disbelief. It is not a deft synonym for *incredible.*

INFER

See **imply, infer.**

INFLAMMABLE

See **flammable, inflammable.**

INGENIOUS, INGENUOUS

What a difference one letter makes. *Ingenious* refers to worldly brilliance; *ingenuous* refers to otherworldly innocence.

IN ORDER TO

Sometimes *in order to* is necessary, but it's often just a fussy way of saying *to: We should exercise in order to stay healthy.* Drop *in order* whenever possible.

IN REGARD(S) TO, WITH REGARD(S) TO

In regard to and *with regard to* are phrases that mean "regarding," "concerning," "on the subject of."

As regards—note the *s* on the end—means the same thing. Perhaps this is why people mindlessly pluralize *regard* and say *in regards to* and its partner in crime, *with regards to.*

Both of the following examples are correct: *With regard to your friend, let's hope she is well.* Compare that to *With regards to your friend. Let's hope she is well.*

In the first sentence, *With regard to* means "concerning." But in the second sentence, *regards* with an *s* is a plural noun meaning "best wishes."

INSURE

See **assure, ensure, insure.**

IRONY

When something is *ironic*, it has a grimly humorous or paradoxical twist, as if the universe were playing a wicked practical joke. Thus, it is *ironic* if a speeding car crashes into a "drive carefully" sign, or if someone named Joe Friendly turns out to be a serial killer.

Do not use *irony* or *ironic* to describe a simple coincidence: *It's so ironic that our birthdays fall on the same day*. No irony there; it's merely *coincidental*.

IRREGARDLESS

This nonsense word results from confusing and combining *regardless* and *irrespective*. If people would just think about it, what's that silly *ir-* doing there?

In technical terms, *ir-* is an **initial negative particle**. So if *irregardless* means anything, it means "not regardless" when the person using it is trying to say the exact opposite.

IS IS

*The thing is is that…The truth is is that…The problem is is that…*The airwaves are teeming with commentators afflicted with the *is is* hiccup, one of life's mysteries, even to those who say it. The most alarming case in point: *The fact of the matter is is that*, a bloated locution intoned by certain pundits, often right before they express an opinion.

ISLE

See **aisle, isle**.

IT'S, ITS

It's: a contraction for *it is* or *it has*.
Its: a possessive pronoun meaning "belonging to it."

J

JELL

See **gel, jell**.

JIBE, JIVE

The verb *jibe* means "to fit," "to be in harmony with": *His version did not jibe with hers*.

Many people say *jive* when they mean *jibe*, but *jive*, noun and verb, is African-American slang that originally referred to up-tempo, jazzy music. Then it became a term for hipster jargon.

It has come to mean dishonesty, silliness, or inanity: *talking jive* is lying or talking nonsense. *Stop jiving* means "Stop fooling around."

JUST

Be careful where you put it. The meaning of *just* depends on its placement in a sentence, especially when it is accompanied by *not*, or by negative verbs such as *don't* or *wouldn't*.

Many people say *just not* when they mean *not just*, and this could lead to misunderstanding, embarrassment, even hurt feelings.

Not just means "not only," whereas *just not* means "simply not" or "definitely not."

He's a trusted adviser, not just a friend means "He's more than an adviser; he's a friend, too." But *He's a trusted adviser, just not a friend* means something quite different: "I trust his advice, but he's no friend of mine."

JUST DESERTS

See **desert, dessert**.

K

KARAT

See **carat, caret, karat**.

KINDERGARTNER

Note how the spelling differs from *kindergarten*.

KNEW, NEW

Knew: past tense of *know*.
New: up to date; original; unused.

KUDOS

To this great man, kudos are due. That sentence wouldn't raise many eyebrows, but *kudos* is not the plural of *kudo*. There's no such thing as "a kudo." *Kudos* is a Greek word (pronounced "KYOO-doss" or "KOO-doss") meaning "praise" or "glory," and you'd no more say "kudos are due" than you'd say "glory are due." Admittedly, *kudos is due* looks odd. Better to rewrite the sentence.

L

LASTLY

If you wouldn't say "firstly," why say "lastly"? Drop the -ly. (See also **secondly, thirdly, fourthly**.)

LATTER

He offered a trip to New York, Chicago, or Tarzana. She chose the latter. Oh no she didn't. *Latter* can't be used when there are three (or more) options. It applies only to sentences like *He offered a trip to New York or Tarzana*, which makes New York the *former*, Tarzana the *latter*. When there are more than two people or things mentioned, use *last*.

LAXADAISICAL

The word doesn't exist, but that doesn't stop people from saying it. The word they're looking for is *lackadaisical*: "without energy or enthusiasm."

LAY, LIE

These may well be the two most confounding three-letter words in all the language. The use of *lay* where *lie* is indicated has been a major problem for generations. Maybe because of the word's negative double meaning, people shy away from saying *lie*.

All of the following are incorrect: *I'm going to lay on the couch. Your wallet is laying on the dresser. He wants to lay down.* Make it *lie, lying, lie*, respectively.

Lie: You *lie* down today; you *lay* down yesterday; you have *lain* down before.

Lay: Please *lay* the book down now; you *laid* the book down yesterday; you have *laid* that book down before.

- *Yesterday I lied/laid/lain/lay on the bed.*
  Most people would guess *laid on the bed*, but the correct answer is *lay*.

- *I have often lied/laid/lain/lay on the bed.*
  Again, most people would guess *laid*, but *lain* is correct.

- *I have often lied/laid/lain/lay my wallet on the dresser.*
  This time, *laid* is correct.

Lay vs. Lie Chart

	Present	**Past**
To recline	*lie; is/are lying*	*lay; has/have/had lain*
To put or place	*lay; is/are laying*	*laid; has/have/had laid*
To tell a falsehood	*lie; is/are lying*	*lied; has/have/had lied*

Examples in the present tense:	*I like to lie down for a nap at 2 p.m.*
	I am lying down for a nap today.
	Please lay the book down.
	I am laying the book down.
	I am tempted to lie about my age.
	I am not lying about my age.
Examples in the past tense:	*I lay down for a nap yesterday at 2 p.m.*
	I laid the book down yesterday.
	He lied on the witness stand.
Examples with a helping verb (**has, have**):	*I have lain down for a nap every day this week.*
	I have laid the book down for the last time.
	He has lied each day on the witness stand.

LEAD, LED

Correct: *He led the parade.* Incorrect: *He lead the parade.* Budding writers are increasingly using *lead* instead of *led* as the past tense of the verb *to lead*.

There are three reasons for this confusion. First, the past tense of *read*, the other common *-ead* verb, is *read*. Second, the word *lead*, when it's a noun denoting a metal, is pronounced *led*, just like the past tense of the verb *to lead*. And third, they don't drill spelling in schools the way they used to.

LEAK, LEEK

Leak: an unintended discharge of liquid or gas.
Leek: a type of onion.

LESS

See **fewer, less**.

LESSEN, LESSON

Lessen: to decrease.
Lesson: something learned or studied.

LET HE WHO IS WITHOUT SIN...

One of the most notorious misquotations in the English language is "Let he who is without sin among you cast the first stone." This misuse of the pronoun *he* has been giving English sticklers nightmares for decades.

How could it be "Let he"? It couldn't. Here is the actual quotation from the Gospel of John: "He that is without sin among you, let him first cast a stone at her."

LIABLE, LIBEL, LIKELY

Liable has a negative connotation: *He's liable to have an accident if he doesn't slow down.*
Libel is a malicious attack on someone's character.
Likely refers to simple probability: *She is likely to be on time.*

LIE

See **lay, lie**.

LIGHTENING, LIGHTNING

That flash in an overcast sky is a bolt of *lightning*, which is sometimes misspelled *lightening*.
Lightening is the process of making something lighter in color or weight.

LIKE

Do it like she does. Sentences like that one have always been unacceptable to purists. Nowadays, however, such sentences go virtually unchallenged, even by many editors.

Strictly speaking, *like* can only be a preposition meaning "similar to" or "similarly to." So *Do it like her* (i.e., *similarly to her*) would be correct. But because no one would say, "Do it similarly to she does," there is no grammatical justification for *Do it like she does.*

In the mid-twentieth century, Theodore M. Bernstein said in *The Careful Writer*: "The usage of *like* as a conjunction...is not acceptable in better-grade writing."

The *American Heritage Dictionary*'s panel of experts has noted that for more than a century, anyone who said *like she does* was considered illiterate. Yet today, the panel says, "*Like* is more acceptably used as a conjunction in informal style."

The traditional view is that if a verb follows the noun or pronoun, as in *like she does*, it means *like* is the wrong choice. Instead, use *as, as if, as though,* or *the way.*

- *Do it **the way** she does* (not *like she does*).
- *Say it **as if** or **as though** you mean it* (not *like you mean it*).
- *Go when the light is green, **as** it is now* (not *like it is now*).

LITERALLY

I was so amazed, I literally hit the ceiling. If someone has *literally* hit the ceiling, he ought to move to a place with higher ceilings.

It was literally like being in Paris. Drop *literally*. Nothing is "literally like." Anyone who says "literally like" doesn't understand the word.

Literally is supposed to mean "100 percent fact"…period. But not today, when, as in the previous examples, *literally* is often used figuratively. That way madness lies.

In responsible usage, *literally* allows no room for poetry, analogy, hyperbole, frivolity, or any other flights of fancy. Any sentence containing *literally* should mean what it literally says. We are being asked to accept that sentence as fact and not interpret or infer. So if you say you were "literally stunned," we have no choice but to conclude that you were physically incapacitated.

A newspaper item told of a couple whose dreams "literally collapsed" when a fixer-upper they bought came down in a heap as they started working on it. Now, we know what the writer meant, but the house is what literally collapsed, not the dreams. How could a dream, the very essence of all that is beyond materiality, *literally* collapse?

One simple solution: Say "virtually": *I virtually hit the ceiling. Their dreams virtually collapsed.*

Virtually allows speakers and writers to enhance and embellish to their hearts' content, options they relinquish when using *literally*.

LOAN, LONE

Loan: something given temporarily.
Lone: only; solitary.

LOATH, LOATHE

Loath: reluctant.
Loathe: to dislike intensely.
I am *loath* to work for anyone I *loathe*.

LOOSE, LOSE

Loose: opposite of *tight*.
Lose: to misplace; to be defeated.

M

MAIL, MALE

Mail: correspondence.
Male: masculine.

MAIZE, MAZE

Maize: corn.

Maze: a labyrinth.

MANNER, MANOR

Manner: a method; a behavior.

Manor: a palatial residence.

MARQUEE, MARQUIS

Marquee: a projection over a theater entrance.

Marquis: an aristocrat; a nobleman.

MARRY, MERRY

Marry: to wed.

Merry: cheerful.

MARSHAL, MARTIAL

Marshal: a law officer (noun). To assemble (verb). Note the spelling: one *l*.

Martial: warlike.

MASTERFUL, MASTERLY

Another pair of words whose distinct meanings have been blurred by carelessness. The problem centers on *masterful*, in such phrases as *a masterful artist* or *a masterful performance*. Make it *masterly*, which means "highly accomplished," "inspired," "demonstrating mastery."

Masterful has darker shadings. It's about being the alpha dog: dominant, supreme—almost ruthlessly so. A *masterful performance* should refer to a boxer or a victorious football team rather than a cello concert.

MATERIAL, MATERIEL

Material: whatever something is made from.

Materiel: military equipment and supplies.

MAY

See **can, may**.

MEDAL, MEDDLE, METAL, METTLE

Medal: a decoration; a badge.

Meddle: to interfere.

Metal: an earth element.
Mettle: boldness; grit.

MEDIA

Among the language's most abused words is *media*, a plural noun; *medium* is the singular. A *medium* is a system of mass communication: *The medium of television is a prominent component of the mass media.*

Every day we hear and read statements like "The media is irresponsible," "The media has a hidden agenda." In those sentences, "media" should be followed by "are" and "have."

There are some who prefer and defend "the media is" and "the media has." To them, the various means of mass communication—newspapers, radio, TV, magazines, blogs, etc.—make up one "media."

The United States **is** *where I live* is correct, even though "States" is plural, so why not "the media is," even though *media* is plural? Nice try, but no sale.

Writers should insist on *the media are*. It's important that people think of *the media* as many voices, opinions, and perspectives rather than one monolithic entity.

MERETRICIOUS

A veteran newsman said, "His career is meretricious." He probably meant *meritorious*. Instead, the sentence as it stands is an insult.

When you hear it, the first two syllables echo *merit*, but the similarity to *meritorious* ends there. *Meretricious* means "flashy," "cheap," "tawdry": *The candidate made a meretricious display of piety.*

METAL, METTLE
See **medal, meddle, metal, mettle**.

MIC

Mic is a bogus and clueless abbreviation of *microphone*. For too many decades to count, the word was *mike*. "Ike is good on a mike" went a line from a popular early-1950s song about presidential candidate Dwight D. Eisenhower.

A bicycle is a *bike*, not a "bic." So how is a microphone a "mic"?

MINER, MINOR
Miner: one who works in a mine.
Minor: someone under the legal age of adulthood (noun); of less importance (adjective).

MINUSCULE

Be sure to note that first *u*. A lot of writers think the word is "miniscule." And it makes sense that a word for "tiny" would have a *mini* in it. Don't think *mini*, think *minus*.

MISNOMER

A *misnomer* is a mistake, but not all mistakes are misnomers. The word is wrongly used in this sentence: *It's a misnomer that elephants are afraid of mice.* A *misnomer* is not the same as a *misconception*. The *nome* in the middle is from the Latin *nomen*, meaning "name." A *misnomer* is a mistake in labeling: for instance, calling aluminum foil "tinfoil" or calling a koala a "bear" (it's a marsupial).

If "Lucky" Brown loses his fortune in the stock market and "Speedy" Green blows out his ankle, their respective nicknames become misnomers.

MORAL, MORALE

Moral: a lesson (noun); ethical (adjective).
Morale: spirit; level of enthusiasm.

MORE IMPORTANTLY, MOST IMPORTANTLY

Traditionalists do not accept *importantly* in sentences like *Most importantly, Churchill was a statesman.* Drop the *-ly* and save yourself a superfluous syllable. More important, you'll be using good English.

MORNING, MOURNING

Morning: the start of the day, between night and afternoon.
Mourning: sorrow over a tragedy.

MUSCLE, MUSSEL

Muscle: fibrous tissue; strength.
Mussel: an edible marine bivalve.

N

NAVAL, NAVEL

Naval: pertaining to ships; nautical.
Navel: belly button.

NEITHER...OR

As a conjunction, *neither* often teams with *nor*: "Neither a borrower nor a lender be." The rule many learned in fifth grade was, "Neither...nor, either...or, but never neither...or."

Neither...or is another once-unthinkable faux pas gaining momentum among people who ought to know better. A political adviser's resignation letter read, "This position is not a fit for me, neither personally or professionally." (Make it "either.")

A big-city newspaper editor wrote, "I neither commissioned or approved it." Even editors need editors.

NEW

See **knew, new**.

NEW RECORD

See **all-time record**.

NONPLUSSED

Note the double *s*.

Nonplussed is widely misused as a synonym for *cool* or *unfazed*: *Despite his anxiety, he appeared nonplussed.* Clearly, the writer meant *nonchalant. nonplussed* means the opposite: "confused," "thrown off." *His strange behavior left her nonplussed.*

NOR

See **neither...or**.

NOT JUST

See **just**.

NOTORIETY

A critic wrote: "Burgess gained notoriety with his wildly popular children's books." Another oft-abused word, *notoriety* has somehow become a good thing. But can't you hear the *notorious* in *notoriety*? There are all kinds of fame; *notoriety* is one of the bad kinds, just down the pike from *infamy*. This is a word best reserved for describing the world's scoundrels.

NUMBER

See **amount, number**.

O

OFF OF

"Hey! You! Get off of my cloud," sang the Rolling Stones, unnecessarily. Make it *off my cloud*. The *of* in "off of" adds nothing, so why not drop it?

ORAL

See **aural, oral**.

ORDINANCE, ORDNANCE

Ordinance: a law.
Ordnance: military weapons and ammunition.

OVERDO, OVERDUE

Overdo: to go overboard with; behave excessively.
Overdue: behind time; payable.

OVERLY

She is overly concerned about her job. Note that if the opposite were true, no one would say "underly concerned." Make it *too concerned* or *overconcerned*.

Many writers think *overly* is unnecessary and a bit precious. "Making *over* into *overly*," says *Bryson's Dictionary of Troublesome Words*, "is a little like turning *soon* into *soonly*. Adding *-ly* does nothing for *over* that it could not already do."

P

PAIL, PALE

Pail: a bucket.
Pale: lacking color.

PAIN, PANE

Pain: physical or emotional suffering.
Pane: a glazed piece or section of a door, window, etc.

PALATE, PALETTE, PALLET

Palate: the roof of the mouth; taste.

Palette: a range of colors; a board to hold and mix paint colors.

Pallet: a low, portable platform.

PARISH, PERISH

Parish: a district with its own church and clergy.

Perish: to stop existing; to die.

PARODY, SATIRE

A *parody* is a humorous imitation of a book, film, song, poem, etc., meant to poke fun at the original's style or intentions.

A *satire* uses biting humor, hyperbole, sarcasm, irony, etc., to lay bare the toxic absurdity of civilization.

PASSED, PAST

Passed: gone ahead of; approved.

Past: a former time; beyond.

PAST HISTORY

A curious term for *history*.

PASTIME, PAST TIME

A *pastime* is a leisurely pursuit or hobby.

The phrase *past time* refers to something that should have happened or been done by now. It's *past time* that people realized that *pastime* is one word.

PEACE, PIECE

Peace: tranquility.

Piece: a portion.

PEAK, PEEK, PIQUE

Peak: a summit.

Peek: a glance (noun); to steal a glance (verb).

Pique: ill humor (noun); to arouse or annoy (verb).

PEAL, PEEL

Peal: to ring.

Peel: to strip.

PEDAL, PEDDLE

Pedal: a foot-activated lever (noun); to operate something with pedals, such as a bicycle or organ (verb).

Peddle: to sell or publicize.

PEER, PIER

Peer: a person who is an equal (noun); to look attentively (verb).

Pier: a structure extending out over water.

PENULTIMATE

"He's the penultimate Washington insider," said the glib pundit, blissfully unaware that *penultimate* means "second to last."

PERCENT

One word.

PERPETRATE, PERPETUATE

Perpetrate: to commit a crime.

Perpetuate: to prolong or sustain.

PERSECUTE, PROSECUTE

To *persecute* is to go after in an intimidating, bullying manner.

To *prosecute* is to go after in a legal manner.

PERSUADE

See **convince, persuade**.

PHASE

See **faze, phase**.

PHENOMENON

This troublemaker baffles even articulate speakers. And they know it. If you listen closely, you'll notice people trying to save face by fudging the last syllable.

Phenomenon is singular. "Management is a universal phenomenon," declares a business website. It helps to remember the *-on* on the end, which almost spells *one*.

The plural form is *phenomena*. A commentator on national television had it exactly backward. He spoke of "the phenomena of climate change" and later used *phenomenon* as a plural. Others say "phenomenas" when they mean *phenomena*.

PIECE

See **peace, piece**.

PIQUE

See **peak, peek, pique**.

PISTIL, PISTOL

Pistil: the female organ of a flower.
Pistol: a gun.

PLAIN, PLANE

Plain: a treeless area of land (noun); not fancy; evident (adjectives).
Plane: a flat or level surface; short form of *airplane*.

PLUM, PLUMB

Plum: a type of fruit.
Plumb: to examine (verb); upright; vertical (adjectives); totally; precisely (adverbs).

p.m.

See **a.m., p.m.**

POINT IN TIME

At that point in time is an exercise in empty pomposity, made (in)famous by the Watergate hearings of the early 1970s and still going strong. Why not just *at that point* or *at that time*?

POLE, POLL

Pole: a long, cylindrical piece of wood or metal.
Poll: a collection of opinions; a survey.

POOR, PORE, POUR

Poor: deprived.
Pore: a small opening (noun). To study carefully (verb).

Pour: to send liquid flowing.

Be careful not to say "pour over" if you mean *pore over*.

PRAY, PREY

Pray: to speak to a deity.

Prey: a victim (noun); to hunt, to exploit (verbs).

PRECIPITATE, PRECIPITOUS

Media pundits have errantly decided that *precipitous* means "immediate" or "swift," as when they discuss the advisability of "precipitous troop withdrawal." The correct adjective would be *precipitate*.

Precipitous means "steep," like a precipice.

PREDOMINATELY

Some mistakenly use it as an alternative to *predominantly*, as in "chiefly," "primarily." Funny thing about *predominately*: you might not see it for long stretches, and then, like some verbal swine flu, it crops up everywhere for a few weeks. Although *predominately* is technically a word, it's not easy to pinpoint what it means.

PREMIER, PREMIERE

Premier is generally an adjective meaning "the best," "of unsurpassed quality, skill, or importance." As a noun, it refers to a head of government.

A *premiere* is an opening night or first performance.

PRESENTLY

Careful speakers and writers might consider avoiding this word. If you tell hungry guests, "We're serving dinner presently," they might think you mean *now*. But *presently* means "in the near future." It's a stuffy word anyway; what's wrong with *soon*?

PRESUME

See **assume, presume**.

PRINCIPAL, PRINCIPLE

Principal: a major participant; the head of an institution (nouns); of first importance; chief (adjectives).

Principle: a fundamental belief; a fundamental fact.

PROFIT, PROPHET

Profit: gain.

Prophet: a predictor; a seer.

PRONE, SUPINE

The victim was found lying prone, her eyes gazing sightlessly at a full moon. Sorry, but this is a maneuver only the swivel-headed girl from *The Exorcist* could pull off, because when you're *prone*, you're lying on your stomach. Make that *supine*, which means "lying on one's back."

PROPHECY, PROPHESIZE, PROPHESY

A *prophecy* is a prediction.

When prophets make prophecies, they *prophesy*, not "prophesize."

It will be a crowning achievement, prophesized its chief engineer. Lose that *z* and make it *prophesied*. It is doubtful you could find any dictionary anywhere that lists "prophesize." Even the nonjudgmental *Webster's New World College Dictionary* shuns this common (mis)usage.

PROSECUTE

See **persecute, prosecute**.

PURPOSELY, PURPOSEFULLY

These words share much common ground, and they are sometimes interchangeable, but there are distinct differences. *Purposely* means "intentionally," but some acts are intentional, yet pointless: *Little Jimmy purposely threw Alice's lunch in the mud.*

Someone who does something *purposefully* is on a mission, with an important goal in mind: *The rescue team purposefully combed the woods for the missing child.*

Q-R

QUOTATION, QUOTE

To purists, *quote* is a verb only. When we *quote*, we repeat or reproduce someone's exact words.

The correct term for quoted material is a *quotation*. In casual usage, a quotation is often called a "quote," but *quote* as a noun is still not acceptable in formal writing.

RACK, WRACK

As a verb, *rack* means "to afflict," "oppress," "torment."

To *wrack* is to cause the ruin of.

A lot of people mistakenly write things like "nerve-wracking" and "I wracked my brains." Drop the *w* in both cases. Both expressions derive from that device in the torture hall of fame called the *rack*.

RAISE, RAZE

Raise: to lift up.

Raze: to take down.

RAP, WRAP

Rap: a sharp blow; a type of music (nouns); to strike sharply (verb).

Wrap: to enclose in a covering.

REAL, REEL

Real: actual, authentic.

Reel: a spool (noun); to stumble; falter (verbs).

REASON BEING IS

One hears this odd phrase frequently, in statements like *The economy is in trouble; the reason being is profligate spending.* Make it either *the reason being profligate spending* or *the reason is profligate spending.*

REASON IS BECAUSE

The reason is because we spend too much. Make it *The reason is that we spend too much.* Saying *the reason is* makes *because* unnecessary.

REEK, WREAK

Reek: to smell bad.

Wreak: to inflict.

REFER

See **allude, elude, refer**.

REGARDLESS

See **irregardless**.

REIGN, REIN

Reign: period in power (noun); to be in power (verb).
Rein: a strap to control horses (noun); to control or guide (verb).

RELISH IN

Jones is relishing in his new role as financial adviser. The sentence mistakes *relish* for *revel*. Either Jones *relishes* his role or he *revels in* his role.

RENOWN

Ansel Adams is renown for his timeless photographs. Make that *renowned*. This widespread gaffe results from thinking *renown* is akin to *known*, probably because they share those last four letters.

REST, WREST

Rest: to relax.
Wrest: to take forcibly.

REST, AS THEY SAY, IS HISTORY

The rest, as they say, is history is a cringe-inducing cliché. Not *The rest is history*, which has its place—it's that pseudo-sagacious *as they say* which really rankles. How to explain the enduring appeal of something so tired, weak, and breathtakingly unoriginal?

RESTAURATEUR

Note the spelling: no *n*.

RETCH, WRETCH

Retch: to heave.
Wretch: a lowly being; a scoundrel.

RETICENT

Reticent means "uncommunicative, reserved, silent." But many people wrongly use it to mean "reluctant": *I was reticent to spend so much on a football game.* No, you were *reticent* when you didn't protest the ticket price.

REVEREND

In formal writing, there's no such thing as "a reverend." The word is an honorific used before a pastor's name: *the Reverend Josiah Blank.* Important: *the* is mandatory. Also note the phrase must be followed by the person's full name—to say "Reverend Blank" is wrong twice.

REVIEW, REVUE

Review: an examination or criticism (noun); to assess, to analyze (verbs).
Revue: a variety show.

RIFF, RIFT

Riff: a brief musical phrase; pithy or flippant wordplay.
Rift: a crack; a disagreement.

RIGHT, RITE, WRITE

Right: an entitlement (noun); correct, opposite of *left*, opposite of *wrong* (adjectives).
Rite: a ritual; a ceremony.
Write: to compose letters or words.

RING, WRING

Ring: the sound of a bell; jewelry worn around a finger.
Wring: to twist.

ROAD, RODE, ROWED

Road: a street; a path; a highway.
Rode: past tense of *ride*.
Rowed: past tense of *row*.

ROLE, ROLL

Role: a position; a part in a play or film.
Roll: a baked food; a flowing movement (nouns); to rotate; to flow with a current (verbs).

RYE, WRY

Rye: a grain.
Wry: mocking; ironic; droll.

S

SATIRE

See **parody, satire**.

SAVER, SAVOR

Saver: someone or something that saves or conserves.
Savor: to appreciate.

SCENT, SENT

Scent: an aroma; a fragrance.
Sent: taken; moved.

SECONDLY, THIRDLY, FOURTHLY

As noted earlier, few people say "firstly," and fewer yet say "fifthly," "sixthly," "seventeenthly," etc. Many adverbs do not end in *-ly*. It makes more sense to use *second, third,* and *fourth* rather than *secondly, thirdly,* and *fourthly*.

SEMIANNUAL

See **biannual, biennial, semiannual**.

SENSUAL, SENSUOUS

Sensual: relating to sexual pleasure.
Sensuous: relating to or affecting the physical senses.

SERF, SURF

Serf: a slave.
Surf: waves.

SERIAL

See **cereal, serial**.

SET, SIT

Set: to place something somewhere.
Sit: to take a seat.

SEW, SO, SOW

Sew: to stitch.

So: as a result; in the manner indicated.

Sow: to scatter or plant seed.

SHEAR, SHEER

Shear: to cut; to clip.

Sheer: pure; steep; translucent.

[*sic*]

This is found only in a direct quotation (note the brackets). An editor inserts [*sic*] directly after a word or sentence to notify readers that something is off or incorrect, but is being reproduced exactly as it originally appeared.

SIGHT

See **cite, sight, site**.

SIMPLISTIC

It's not the same as *simple*. It means "oversimplified," as in *Your simplistic argument leaves out too many facts*.

At a memorial service, a well-meaning soul remembered a renowned artist as "a simplistic man." Some occasions are too solemn for foolish language lapses. Trying to express something commendable, the speaker instead said the dear departed had been a simpleton.

SINCE

See **because, since**.

SITE

See **cite, sight, site**.

SLASH

Despite its popularity, the slash (/), technically known as a **virgule**, is frowned on by purists. Other than to indicate dates (*9/11/2001*) or separate lines of poetry ("Celery, raw / Develops the jaw"), it has few defensible uses in formal writing.

Usually a hyphen, or in some cases the word *or*, will suffice. Instead of writing *the novelist/poet Eve Jones*, make it *the novelist-poet Eve Jones*. Rather than *available to any man/woman who is qualified*, make it *any man or woman*.

"The virgule is a mark that doesn't appear much in first-rate writing," says Bryan A. Garner in *A Dictionary of Modern American Usage*. "Use it as a last resort."

SLEIGHT, SLIGHT

Sleight: dexterity; skill.
Slight: slender; of little substance.

SNUCK

Many think *snuck* is the past tense of *sneak*, but it's not, at least not yet. The past tense of *sneak* is *sneaked*.

SO

See **sew, so, sow**.

SOAR, SORE

Soar: to fly high.
Sore: painful; in pain.

SOLE, SOUL

Sole: the bottom of a foot; a type of fish (nouns); single; solitary (adjectives).
Soul: essence; the spirit apart from the body.

SOME, SUM

Some: an unspecified number.
Sum: the total from adding numbers.

SON, SUN

Son: male offspring.
Sun: the star that is the central body of our solar system.

SOW

See **sew, so, sow**.

STAID, STAYED

Staid: solemn; serious.
Stayed: remained; waited.

STAIR, STARE

Stair: a step.
Stare: to gaze intently.

STAKE, STEAK

Stake: a wager; an investment; a pole.
Steak: a cut of meat.

STATIONARY, STATIONERY

Stationary: in one place; inactive.
Stationery: writing paper.

STEAL, STEEL

Steal: to rob.
Steel: an iron alloy (noun); to toughen (verb).

STEP, STEPPE

Step: a stair (noun); to move by lifting the foot (verb).
Steppe: vast grassland.

STOMPING GROUNDS

It started out as *stamping grounds*, which is still preferred by most dictionaries.

STRAIGHT, STRAIT

Words like *straitjacket* and *strait-laced* are frequently misspelled using *straight*, which is incorrect, but understandable. Wouldn't a "straightjacket" be just the thing to straighten you up and straighten you out? Doesn't "straight-laced" aptly describe a person of refinement (the *lace* part) who lives the "straight life"? This is why some authorities accept *straight-laced* as an alternative spelling. But a *strait* is a narrow channel, and it is that sense of "confinement with little room to maneuver" that generated these terms.

STRATEGY, STRATAGEM

Note the second *a* in *stratagem*.

Both words refer to plans of action. But *stratagem* denotes trickery. It is a scheme to deceive or outwit.

SUM

See **some, sum**.

SUN

See **son, sun**.

SUNDAE, SUNDAY

Sundae: ice cream with syrup.

Sunday: a day of the week.

SUPINE

See **prone, supine**.

SUPPOSE TO

Never "suppose to." Don't drop the *d* in usages like *You're supposed to be here.*

SURF

See **serf, surf**.

SYMPATHY

See **empathy, sympathy**.

T

TACK, TACT

Tack and *tact* are commonly confused when discussing strategy.

A *tack* is a course of action.

Tact is discretion.

We decided to try a new tack is correct, but "a new tact" is what a lot of people say, mistakenly thinking "tact" is short for *tactic*.

TAIL, TALE

Tail: the hindmost animal appendage.
Tale: a story.

TAKE

See **bring, take**.

TAUGHT, TAUT

Taught: trained; educated.
Taut: stiff; tightly stretched.

TEAM, TEEM

Team: a group with the same goal (noun); to form a squad (verb).
Teem: to swarm.

TEMBLOR

Although it produces tremors and makes the ground tremble, an earthquake is a *temblor*, not a "tremblor."

TENANT, TENET

A *tenant* is someone who pays rent to use or occupy a property. But "tenant" is often mistakenly used in place of *tenet*, a fundamental belief or principle held true by a group or organization.

THAN, THEN

Than is used for comparison.
Then means "next," "after that."

THAT

See **who, which, that**.

THEIR, THERE, THEY'RE

Their: belonging to them.
There: in that place.

They're: contraction of *they are*.
They're in *their* car over *there*.

THOSE KIND OF

Instead of "those kind of things," say either *those kinds of things* or *things of that kind*. Better yet: *things like that*.

TILL, 'TIL

Always use *till*. You won't find a reference book anywhere that recommends *'til*. Writer John B. Bremner declares brusquely, "Either *till* or *until*, but not *'til*."

It's natural to assume that *'til* is a contraction of *until*. However, *till* predates *until* by several centuries.

TO, TOO, TWO

To: in the direction of; toward.
Too: also; excessively.
Two: the number after *one*.

TORT, TORTE

Tort: a breach of contract.
Torte: a rich cake made with little or no flour.

TORTUOUS, TORTUROUS

Tortuous: winding; twisting: *a tortuous trail*.
Torturous: painful; causing suffering: *held under torturous conditions*.

TOTALLY

Not to be used arbitrarily. How is *totally convinced* different from *convinced*?

TOWARD, TOWARDS

The *Associated Press Stylebook* insists on *toward*, but both are acceptable and mean the same thing.

TRANSPIRE

The celebrity issued a statement through his attorney that he was "sorry and saddened over what transpired." This usage of *transpire*, though common, is incorrect. The word doesn't mean "occur" or "happen." Something that transpires is revealed or becomes known over time. The Oxford online dictionary gives this example: "It transpired that millions of dollars of debt had been hidden in a complex web of transactions."

TREMBLOR

See **temblor**.

TROOP, TROUPE

Troop: a body of soldiers.

Troupe: a group of traveling performers.

Mike is a real trouper. Many would spell it "trooper." But a *trooper* is either a cop or a soldier in the cavalry, whereas a *trouper*, according to the *American Heritage Dictionary*, is "a reliable, uncomplaining, often hard-working person."

TRULY

Note the spelling: no *e*.

This word is often just window dressing. How is *I truly believe* different from *I believe?*

TURBID, TURGID

Turbid means "muddy," or "unclear," literally and figuratively. Both a river and a poem may properly be called turbid.

Turgid means "swollen," literally and figuratively. One may suffer physically from a turgid limb, or mentally from a turgid (i.e., pompous and bombastic) speech.

U

UNINTERESTED

See **disinterested, uninterested**.

UNIQUE

The Big Easy is one of America's most unique cities. Drop *most*. What's wrong with saying *one of America's unique cities?*

Unique is, on its own, a potent word, and it must never be accompanied by an intensifier, since modifying it saps its considerable power. When you use *unique*, put it out there alone—otherwise, say *unusual*.

Unique belongs to a group of words called **absolutes** or **incomparables**. Examples include *dead, equal, essential, eternal, opposite, supreme*. Such words resist being modified. Modifiers like *more, most, absolutely, rather*, and *very* either strip them of their strength or result in foolishness.

"Would you say 'very one-of-a-kind'?" asks Roy Blount Jr. in his book *Alphabet Juice*. Adding *very* or *absolutely* to *unique*, Blount says, "is like putting a propeller on a rabbit to make him hop better."

UTILIZE

All the way back in the 1940s, George Orwell blew the whistle on this pretentious word in his classic essay "Politics and the English Language." Orwell advised writers to get over themselves and go with *use*. But *use* is so humble, so mundane, whereas *utilize* really sounds like something. Bureaucrats in particular love to use *utilize*.

V

VAIN, VANE, VEIN

Vain: futile; narcissistic.
Vane: a blade moved by wind: *weather vane*.
Vein: a blood vessel; a mood.

VENAL, VENIAL

Venal: corrupt," "able and willing to be bribed."
Venial: "forgivable."

Any writer who inadvertently drops the *i* in a sentence like *Her lapse was venial* may want to think about getting a good lawyer.

VERSES, VERSUS

Verses: lines of poetry.
Versus: as compared to another choice; against.

VERY

Serious writers are wary of *very*. Very often, this very word is very unnecessary.

VIABLE

Viable means "able or fit to live": *viable cells, a viable fetus.*

In popular usage, *viable* has become synonymous with *possible, workable, feasible*. Many purists consider this unacceptable. Roy Copperud, in *American Usage and Style*, says "the word has had the edge hopelessly ground off it."

VIAL, VILE

Vial: a small container.
Vile: evil, depraved.

VICE, VISE

Vice: a bad habit; an immoral practice.
Vise: a device used to hold an object firmly.

VIRTUALLY

See **literally**.

W

WAIST, WASTE

Waist: the part of the human body between the ribs and hips.
Waste: garbage (noun); to squander (verb); to spend uselessly (verb).

WAIT, WEIGHT

Wait: to stay; to be available.
Weight: heaviness; significance.

WAIVER, WAVER

Waiver: relinquishment of a right.
Waver: to feel indecisive; to swing unsteadily.

WARN, WORN

Warn: to notify about trouble.
Worn: carried on the body; deteriorated.

WARRANTEE, WARRANTY

Warrantee: a person who is given a written guarantee or a warrant.
Warranty: a written guarantee.

WARY, WEARY

Wary: mistrustful; guarded.
Weary: exhausted; drained.

WAY, WEIGH

Way: a method; a direction; a manner.

Weigh: to measure mass; to mull over.

WAYS TO GO

A ways to go, meaning "a considerable distance," is best avoided in formal writing.

WEAK, WEEK

Weak: lacking strength.

Week: a period of seven days.

WEATHER, WHETHER

Weather: climatic conditions (noun); to withstand (verb).

Whether: if; in case.

WHETHER OR NOT

Often, the *or not* can be dropped, as in *I don't know whether or not you've heard this.*

WHICH

See **who, which, that**.

WHILE, WILE

While: during.

Wile: a ploy to fool, trap, or entice.

WHO, WHICH, THAT

Use *who* only when referring to humans. Avoid such usages as *a company who* or *a country who* or *a dog who*. For those, *that* or *which* is correct.

Contrary to superstition, *that* is perfectly acceptable when applied to people. *The Man That Got Away* and *The Girl That I Marry*, two hit ballads from the mid-twentieth century, were written at a time when the popular culture expected literacy from its songwriters. And don't forget the famous quotation from the Gospel of John which begins, "He that is without sin among you..."

Which as a pronoun should never refer to humans. (It's an adjective in sentences like *Which man do you mean?*)

WHOLE

See **hole, whole**.

WHOLLY

See **holy, wholly**.

WHO'S, WHOSE

Who's is a contraction of *who is* or *who has*.
Whose is the possessive case of *who*.
Who's the man whose wife called?

WITH REGARD(S) TO

See **in regard(s) to, with regard(s) to**.

WON'T, WONT

Won't: contraction of *will not*.
Wont: habit; custom (nouns); accustomed (adjective).

WORN

See **warn, worn**.

WRACK

See **rack, wrack**.

WRAP

See **rap, wrap**.

WREAK

See **reek, wreak**.

WREAK (WRECK) HAVOC

Because *wreak havoc* means "to cause destruction," some mistakenly think the first word of the phrase is *wreck*.

WREST

See **rest, wrest**.

WRETCH

See **retch, wretch**.

WRING

See **ring, wring**.

WRITE

See **right, rite, write**.

WRY

See **rye, wry**.

Y

YOKE, YOLK

Yoke: a harness for oxen.

Yolk: the yellow part of an egg.

YOU'RE, YOUR

You're: contraction of *you are*.

Your: belonging to you.

CHAPTER 6

QUIZZES

GRAMMAR *PRETEST*

Correct the grammar error in each sentence. Answers are in Chapter Seven.

Example: *Shoshana felt badly about failing the Geometry test.*
Correction: *Shoshana felt bad about failing the geometry test.*

1. How quick he runs.
2. Neither one of them are ready yet.
3. The desk and the chair sits in the corner.
4. Each of us were scheduled to take the test.
5. The coach, not the players, have been ill.
6. There is only four days until Christmas.
7. She is one of the women who works hard.
8. That was Yusuf and me whom you saw.
9. This phone call is for Bill and I.
10. Terrell is the smartest of the two.
11. It was I whom called.
12. It is us clerks who work hard.
13. He took the plate off of the table.
14. I am doing fine. How about yourself?
15. They mailed the copies to him and I.

16. Neither of the candidates have spoken.

17. How will you be effected financially if downsizing means you will lose your job?

18. Joan walks slow so her children can keep up with her.

19. Jake is the oldest of the two brothers.

20. May did good on the test she took yesterday.

21. He and she were real close friends.

22. Whomever drove in the carpool lane without any passengers will be fined.

23. Please allow Jenna or myself to assist you.

24. It's a company who doesn't judge others by their nationalities and accents.

25. They fought over their father's estate because they felt angrily about the way he had treated them.

26. You look well in that running outfit.

27. Don't feel badly about forgetting my birthday.

28. We saw two puppies at the pound and took home the cutest one.

29. Speak clearer please.

30. Where is that book at?

31. Pollen effects my sinuses and makes me sneeze.

32. I want to lay down for a nap, but the phone keeps ringing.

33. That SUV, that landed on its hood after the accident, was traveling at eighty miles per hour.

34. Yesterday, Barry lay my jacket on the hood of the car.

35. We need to discuss this farther.

36. My daughter became a honorary member of the city council for the day.

37. The group is on their best behavior.

38. Your the only one for me.

39. That redwood tree has become taller then the oak tree next door.

40. The time for action has long since past.

41. Its a long way from here to Tierra del Fuego.

42. Mother, can I go to the movies with Ashton this afternoon?

43. I could of danced all night.

44. Srdjian immigrated from his native Bosnia about five years ago.

45. Did you see the beautiful broach Genevieve was wearing today?

46. The teacher tried to illicit a discussion about the novel.

47. La Donna talks fondly about the four years that she has went to the university.

48. The answer is plane and simple.

49. Let me sit this book down on the table before I answer your question.

50. The legislature finally authorized the funds to polish the gold on the dome of the capital building.

FINDING NOUNS, VERBS, AND SUBJECTS *QUIZ 1*

Underline the subjects once and the verbs twice. Correct the capitalization of nouns if needed. Answers are in Chapter Seven.

> **Example**:   *He arrived at heathrow airport on time.*
> **Answer**:   He <u>arrived</u> at Heathrow Airport on time.

1. The overturned truck blocked both lanes.

2. He appears to be deep in thought.

3. The Metropolitan Museum of Art is a New York city landmark.

4. She will fly part of the way and then drive fifty kilometers to get there.

5. Honesty is the best policy.

6. Get over here quickly!

7. From the bottom of the cave, the stalagmites rose ten feet high.

8. Through the mist, the Bridge appeared.

9. I will just be watching the boston marathon, but my wife will be running in it.

10. Behind the door is a coat rack.

11. Joe has been helping out with the chores.

12. He should have been more gracious.

FINDING NOUNS, VERBS, AND SUBJECTS *QUIZ 2*

Underline the subjects once and the verbs twice. Correct the capitalization of nouns if needed. Answers are in Chapter Seven.

> **Example**:   *She scratched her silver ring against the edge of the pool.*
> **Answer**:   She <u>scratched</u> her silver ring against the edge of the pool.

1. He depends on her in times of need.

2. Watch your step.

3. The Insurance Agent gave her sound advice.

4. On the table was her purse.

5. In the newspaper, an interesting article appeared.

6. Look before you leap.

7. Across the road lived her boyfriend.

8. We are forced to inhale and exhale this smog-filled air.

9. In the gutter, I found a shiny new dime.

10. Around every cloud is a silver lining.

11. How long have you been living in new Delhi?

12. They must have given up eventually.

SUBJECT AND VERB AGREEMENT *QUIZ 1*

Underline the subjects once and the verbs twice. If the subjects and verbs do not agree, change the verbs to match the subjects. Place a check mark in front of sentences that are correct. Answers are in Chapter Seven.

> **Example**:   *Willard and his sister is going for a long hike.*
> **Correction**:   *Willard and his sister are going for a long hike.*

1. That pack of lies are not going to cause me to change my mind.

2. My favorite team's colors are orange and black.

3. Here's two more factors to consider.

4. Neither the rain nor the darkness are going to stop me.

5. My staff believes in providing high-quality service.

6. This is one of the things that bothers me about grammar.

7. Mary Lou asked that he take out the trash.

8. Either the bikes or the lawn mower go in that space.

9. Oh my, there's not enough desserts for everyone.

10. The bag of toys is going to a needy family.

11. Neither my brother nor my sister-in-law are taking Mom to the doctor.

12. The conductor, as well as the musicians, are taking the stage.

13. A majority of the community support lower speed limits.

14. My whole family are vacationing in Baja California this winter.

15. Did he say sixty dollars are the cost of going to the ball game?

16. The distance alone, besides the costs involved, are too great to consider moving.

17. Law and order is the principle he based his campaign on.

18. There's lots of food left.

19. There's lots of people here.

20. If it was up to me, we would leave earlier in the morning.

21. One in three stressed Americans cope by shopping.

22. Four years are considered the normal amount of time to earn a bachelor's degree.

SUBJECT AND VERB AGREEMENT *QUIZ 2*

Underline the subjects once and the verbs twice. If the subjects and verbs do not agree, change the verbs to match the subjects. Place a check mark in front of sentences that are correct. Answers are in Chapter Seven.

Example: *The box of books were opened yesterday.*
Correction: *The* <u>box</u> *of books* <u>was opened</u> *yesterday.*

1. Al and Eli go to the beach to surf with their friends.

2. There's three strawberries left.

3. The group of children from that school has never seen the ocean.

4. If our staff members keep picking at each other, we will not meet our goals.

5. A lot of things she said was the truth.

6. My problem, which is minor in comparison with others, exist because I dropped out of high school.

7. Most of my savings is invested in real estate.

8. She's one of those professionals who really pays attention.

9. Some of my goals has yet to be met.

10. All of my goals are being met and surpassed.

11. None of this is your business.

12. Nervousness, not to mention lack of sleep, contribute to poor performance.

13. One-third of the city are experiencing a blackout tonight.

14. One-third of the people are suffering.

15. The next thing I heard were two shots.

16. Ladies and gentlemen, here's Wisin and Yandel.

17. Neither Darren nor Ida are capable of such a crime.

18. Eighty miles on one charge are the maximum range for my electric car.

19. I wish it were summer and time for vacation.

20. Her attitude is one of the things that's different.

PRONOUNS *QUIZ 1*

Circle the correct word(s) in each sentence. Answers are in Chapter Seven.

1. It is he/him who will be responsible for making all of the arrangements.

2. It is I who is/am wrong.

3. I hope my boss gives that assignment to Laura and I/me.

4. She was one of those cruise passengers who is/are always complaining.

5. Each of the players get/gets to make a speech before the parade.

6. Julia is a faster runner than I/me.

7. The sweater that we found at the church is yours/your's.

8. The dog hurt its/it's paw while running through the empty field.

9. George and I/myself finished staining the deck.

10. Everyone wrote <u>their</u>/<u>his or her</u> own autobiography in the class.

11. She/her and Carlos are the baby's godparents.

12. The honors committee nominated he/him and Ming.

13. Everyone working on this together <u>have</u>/<u>has</u> come to <u>a different conclusion</u>/<u>different conclusions</u>.

14. You more than anyone else knows/know what the risks are.

15. Her/She and I/me are in charge of the sales presentation tomorrow.

16. Neither of the girls are/is planning a wedding in the near future.

17. It is we/us who will get the blame if things do not go well.

18. Its/It's obvious that the best team will prevail.

19. Nora is one of the candidates who is/are worthy of my vote.

20. Nora, of all the candidates who is/are running, is the best.

PRONOUNS *QUIZ 2*

Fix any errors in the following sentences. Place a check mark in front of sentences that are correct. Answers are in Chapter Seven.

1. Meagan said she looked forward to seeing he and I at the airport.

2. Him and me have been good friends since second grade.

3. Yes, this is her speaking.

4. My friend, unlike myself, is very artistic.

5. Please talk to Daniela or myself next time you have a concern.

6. As I've said before, ask either Boris or she, not me.

7. None of the doctors have been able to figure out what is wrong with she or I.

8. She is as stubborn as him, but that's no surprise given they are sister and brother.

9. I weigh more than him.

10. Who's hat is this?

11. It is us who deserves credit for this company's third-quarter profits.

12. Its a shame that some of the profits have been wasted on excessive executive compensation packages.

13. If you have any questions, please call either Randy or myself.

14. Me and my friend will stop by on our way to the bakery.

15. You can help him or me but probably not both of us.

16. It is me who is to blame.

17. My boss and me will pick up where the others left off.

18. When the horse kicked it's legs, the rider landed in the lake.

19. You're friend told her's to tell my friend that their's a party tonight.

20. The argument he gave had it's merits.

WHO, WHOM, WHOEVER, WHOMEVER *QUIZ 1*

Choose the correct word (*who, whom, whoever,* or *whomever*) to complete each sentence. Answers are in Chapter Seven.

1. _____ brought the mail in today?

2. He is the doctor _____ took Jimmy's tonsils out.

3. _____ did you go to the movie with?

4. There will be a prize awarded to _____ finishes first.

5. Fatima was the cashier _____ won the lottery.

6. It does not matter to me _____ drives tomorrow.

7. I will be happy to help _____ needs extra assistance.

8. Sheila will have her hair styled by _____ her friend Rhonda recommends.

9. I will ride with _____ is planning to stop at the store.

10. _____ wrote the story did an excellent job.

11. Next week they will decide _____ will be on the varsity team.

12. Please thank _____ brought in our mail while we were gone.

13. Andre is the person _____ we think is the most qualified.

14. We will hire _____ you trust to do the work.

15. _____ used the grill last forgot to clean it.

16. _____ are you mailing that letter to?

17. I will drive _____ Orlando decides to invite to the game.

18. _____ do you trust to fix your computer?

19. _____ can eat 25 hot wings will win a T-shirt.

20. The wedding florist _____ we wanted to hire is unavailable.

WHO, WHOM, WHOEVER, WHOMEVER *QUIZ 2*

Choose the correct word (*who, whom, whoever,* or *whomever*) to complete each sentence. Answers are in Chapter Seven.

1. _____ is your closest friend?

2. _____ do you bank with?

3. _____ do you think will win the award?

4. Clare knows _____ the winner is already.

5. Omar will talk about his girlfriend with _____ asks him.

6. Kimiko donates her time to _____ she feels needs it most.

7. Quinton will work on the project with _____ you suggest.

8. _____ was that in the clown costume?

9. Kathy was not sure _____ she was voting for.

10. _____ wins the lottery will become a millionaire.

11. He is the man _____ Mr. O'Brian hired.

12. She is the woman _____ I believe was hired last year.

13. _____ were you speaking about just now?

14. _____ do you think will do the work best?

15. I will vote for _____ you think is best.

16. I will vote for _____ you suggest.

17. _____ shall I ask about this matter?

18. Give the information to _____ requests it.

19. Give the information to _____ they prefer.

20. _____ do you suppose runs this show?

WHO, WHOM, THAT, WHICH *QUIZ 1*

Correct *who, whom, that,* or *which* in the following sentences. Place a check mark in front of sentences that are correct. Answers are in Chapter Seven.

1. Tina is looking for a pet **who** is small and easy to care for.

2. Andre was the boy **who** we hired to shovel our snow.

3. The package **which** was left on the porch was our book order.

4. The mechanic **that** fixed my car did a great job.

5. I hope we can find a restaurant **that** we can all agree on.

6. The red vase, **that** she sold for $20, was worth $200.

7. Mike is having a difficult time finding a tutor **who** we can afford.

8. That is the mascara **that** caused my allergic reaction.

9. Was he the only student in the class **who** applied for the scholarship?

10. My favorite store, **which** is closing Friday, is having a big sale.

WHO, WHOM, THAT, WHICH *QUIZ 2*

Correct *who, whom, that,* or *which* in the following sentences. Place a check mark in front of sentences that are correct. Answers are in Chapter Seven.

1. Ahmed is the skydiver **that** broke his back last week.
2. That **that** doesn't kill you makes you stronger.
3. I love hearing the owls **who** sit in the trees and hoot at dusk.
4. The domino theory, **that** stated that when one country fell to communism, others in the area would be likely to fall, was used as an argument to continue the Vietnam War.
5. The game **which** intrigues Gretchen the most is dominoes.
6. Gandhi was a role model **who** millions admired.
7. The tomatoes **which** grow in her garden are unlike those you buy in a store.
8. The tomatoes from her garden, **which** grew larger than those in the grocery store, were sweet and ripe.
9. The baker **who** we hired should win an award.

ADJECTIVES AND ADVERBS *QUIZ 1*

Decide whether the sentences are written correctly. If not, change them. Place a check mark in front of the sentences that are correct. Answers are in Chapter Seven.

1. Allison runs very clumsy.
2. Her boyfriend said she looked good in her new dress.
3. I feel just as badly about this as you do.
4. I did good today on my final exam.
5. C.J. slept sound after running the marathon.
6. Despite her honest efforts, my grandmother's driving is worst than ever.
7. To dance good, you have to practice a lot.
8. Of your three dogs, which is cuter?
9. School policy says that children should stay home from school if they do not feel well.
10. Your house looks similarly to the Johnsons' house.

11. Eat daintier please.
12. Do you like soccer or basketball best?
13. You should speak more careful around my daughter.
14. He still hears good for someone who's played in a rock band for twenty years.
15. His hearing is good for someone who's played in a rock band for twenty years.
16. Our homemade fried rice was real tasty.
17. I think my left eye is my sharpest eye.
18. Dana did not get into her favorite college because her essay was written bad.
19. He looked pensive sitting cross-legged under the willow tree.
20. These days, children don't know how to treat each other nice.

ADJECTIVES AND ADVERBS *QUIZ 2*

Decide whether the sentences are written correctly. If not, change them. Place a check mark in front of the sentences that are correct. Answers are in Chapter Seven.

1. Come quick or we will miss our bus.
2. He swings the bat as good as anyone in major-league baseball.
3. I have never been less surer of anything in my life.
4. Ella was the best of the two sisters at gymnastics.
5. You did that somersault so good.
6. Rochelle felt badly about forgetting Devlin's birthday.
7. This is the worst oil spill I have ever seen.
8. The jasmine has bloomed and smells very sweet.
9. She looked suspiciously to the man wearing the trench coat.
10. She looked suspiciously at the man wearing the trench coat.
11. To find her, we need to follow those set of tracks.
12. Who is the faster runner: Usain, Johan, or Justin?
13. Do you feel happily about your performance on the math quiz?
14. The new model of this chain saw operates much quieter than the old model.
15. She felt good about getting her puppy from the SPCA.
16. You'd better be able to prove that, of all the candidates, you're more qualified.
17. Which is the worst, a toothache or a headache?

18. She reacted swift, which made him feel badly about insulting her.

19. The herbs in the salad tasted bitter.

20. Sharon fought bitterly against her ex-husband for custody of their daughter.

PREPOSITIONS *QUIZ 1*

Correct the following sentences by adding, removing, or changing the prepositions. Place a check mark in front of sentences that are correct. Answers are in Chapter Seven.

1. We could of been there by now if we hadn't gotten lost.
2. Where did you buy that beautiful necklace at?
3. Charles talks like his brother does.
4. He drove his car in the garage.
5. Did you take an envelope off of my desk?
6. Where did Nadia's little dog go to?
7. Like the ranger said, this is an area with a lot of poison ivy.
8. Stacey's copy of the book was different than mine.
9. Jacques acted like he never met your aunt.
10. The tour guide led our group into the library.

PREPOSITIONS *QUIZ 2*

Correct the following sentences by adding, removing, or changing the prepositions. Place a check mark in front of sentences that are correct. Answers are in Chapter Seven.

1. Where did you get this from?
2. I could of danced all night.
3. This problem is no different than many others I've dealt with.
4. The lioness ate like she hadn't eaten food in a week.
5. Take your plate off of the table.
6. Cut the pie up into six slices.
7. I don't know what you are talking about.
8. You could of told me about the mistake earlier.

9. I don't know where he is at, or I would tell you.

10. I'm going to turn this lost wallet into the police.

AFFECT VS. EFFECT *QUIZ 1*

Circle the correct word in each sentence. Answers are in Chapter Seven.

1. Mark told Taneisha that cigarettes would negatively affect/effect her health.

2. The service trip to Central America had a life-altering affect/effect on Rosemary.

3. To affect/effect better treatment of food-packaging laborers, Aaron started a workers union.

4. The convict showed little affect/effect throughout her trial.

5. When the school's new rules take affect/effect, students will no longer be allowed to leave campus during lunch.

6. Do you think our campaign will be affective/effective?

7. Bobby's friends tend to affect/effect his rash decision making.

8. Working overtime at the office negatively affected/effected Keeton's personal life.

9. It is unfortunate that fossil fuels have such a drastic affect/effect on the environment.

10. One must be a powerful speaker to affect/effect social change.

11. Jojo found that meditation had therapeutic affects/effects.

12. The choices we make now will affect/effect society for generations to come.

13. Professor Nguyen's harsh grading had the unintended affect/effect of discouraging interest in the course.

14. The bike safety law currently in affect/effect should be improved.

15. The emergence of social networking websites affected/effected her productivity.

16. Do you think that winning the lottery has affected/effected Jujhaar's personality?

AFFECT VS. EFFECT *QUIZ 2*

Circle the correct word in each sentence. Answers are in Chapter Seven.

1. The affect/effect of the antibiotic on her infection was surprising.

2. I did not know that antibiotics could affect/effect people so quickly.

3. Plastic surgery had an affect/effect not only on her appearance but also on her self-esteem.

4. If the chemotherapy has no affect/effect, should she get surgery for the tumor?

5. When will we know if the chemotherapy has taken affect/effect?

6. Losing her hair from chemotherapy did not affect/effect her as much as her friends had expected.

7. To have the most affect/effect, you should know both your strengths and your weaknesses.

8. The movie *Winged Migration* had two affects/effects on him: he became an environmental advocate and a bird lover.

9. The net affect/effect of blowing the whistle on her boss was that she was eventually given his position.

10. What was the affect/effect of his promotion?

11. His decision affected/effected everyone here.

12. We had to affect/effect a reduction in costs.

13. The critics greatly affected/effected his thinking.

14. How were you able to affect/effect such radical changes?

15. That book had a major affect/effect on his philosophy.

LAY VS. LIE *QUIZ 1*

Make corrections to the words in **bold** where needed. Place a check mark in front of sentences that are correct. Answers are in Chapter Seven.

1. Grandma is not feeling well and went to **lay** down.

2. The mail has **laid** on the table unopened for two days now.

3. The cat will probably be **lying** in the sun after she eats her lunch.

4. The chickens **layed** enough eggs for us to make three large omelets.

5. Bobby has been **lying** his clothes on the bed instead of folding them.

6. The girls **layed** in the tent and pretended they were camping out.

7. Omar **laid** on the air mattress and floated on the water for hours.

8. He forgot where he had **layed** his keys.

9. **Lay** out all the clothes that you want to pack.

10. You should have **lain** out all the clothes that you wanted to pack.

LAY VS. LIE *QUIZ 2*

Make corrections to the words in **bold** where needed. Place a check mark in front of sentences that are correct. Answers are in Chapter Seven.

1. I am dizzy and need to **lay** down.
2. When I got dizzy yesterday, I **laid** down.
3. My brother **lays** carpet for a living.
4. That rug has **lain** there for decades.
5. We need to **lie** this baby down for a nap.
6. We will know we have **lain** this issue to rest when we no longer fight about it.
7. The lions are **laying** in wait for their prey.
8. The lions have **laid** in wait for their prey.
9. I **laid** the blanket over her as she slept.
10. I will **lie** my head on my pillow.

ADVICE VS. ADVISE *QUIZ 1*

Circle the correct word. Answers are in Chapter Seven.

1. My doctor adviced/advised me to go to the gym more often.
2. I always ask my brother for advice/advise because he knows me best.
3. My advice/advise is to talk to Georgia face-to-face, rather than by e-mail.
4. The traffic reporters advice/advise commuters to take the back roads because of the accident on the freeway.
5. If you are interested in becoming a marine biologist, I would advice/advise you to talk to Hank.
6. Even though Scott always gives Eden bad advice/advise, she still follows it.
7. Although Bhaven is not very opinionated, he gives astute advice/advise.
8. Teachers advice/advise parents to emphasize reading at home.
9. When giving advice/advise to a friend, I try to put myself in her shoes.
10. The ride operator advices/advises passengers to keep their limbs inside the roller coaster.

ADVICE VS. ADVISE *QUIZ 2*

Circle the correct word. Answers are in Chapter Seven.

1. Adele is always happy to offer advice/advise if you ask her for it.
2. The lawyer adviced/advised him to plead guilty.
3. If you want to go on the senior trip, I would strongly advice/advise you to start saving your money.
4. Our new members are impressed with the level of advice/advise they received from the leadership group.
5. Sara always takes my advice/advise to heart.
6. I'd like to ask an engineer to advice/advise us on the design.
7. We adviced/advised the city council that the deadline was tentative and might need to be extended.
8. Lakeisha knows she can always go to her best friend for advice/advise.
9. Don't give advice/advise that you're not willing to follow yourself.
10. Randall has a bad habit of offering unsolicited advice/advise.

THEIR VS. THERE VS. THEY'RE *QUIZ 1*

Circle the correct word. Answers are in Chapter Seven.

1. The Garcias are having a costume party at their/there/they're house tonight.
2. I heard that the best beaches are in Southern California, but I would rather not drive all the way down their/there/they're.
3. While their/there/they're in town, we want to show LaDasha and Raquel the beach at sunset.
4. Their/There/They're are many ways to cut a cake.
5. Celia allows her children to watch television once they have finished their/there/they're homework.
6. Paul and Summer are in search of a tank for their/there/they're baby turtles.
7. On Thursday, their/there/they're going to take a paragliding lesson.
8. After a long day of work, their/there/they're brains were fried.

9. Even though their/there/they're is not enough space in my room for that tree, my dad refuses to move it.

10. To our surprise, Nick and Taylor just announced that their/there/they're getting married!

THEIR VS. THERE VS. THEY'RE *QUIZ 2*

Circle the correct word. Answers are in Chapter Seven.

1. According to an old legend, their/there/they're is treasure buried on that island.

2. Juan and Pancho just called to let us know their/there/they're coming for dinner.

3. Their/There/They're is a mouse in my closet!

4. I can't wait to see the looks on their/there/they're faces when I tell them the truth.

5. I wonder if their/there/they're planning to go shopping with us.

6. The children went upstairs to play after clearing their/there/they're plates at dinner.

7. It's their/there/they're decision, so I'll just stay out of it.

8. I don't know what their/there/they're doing to cause all that noise, but it's giving me a headache!

9. The kids haven't called yet; I'm concerned about their/there/they're being out so late at night.

10. I believe Wynona left her glasses over their/there/they're.

MORE CONFUSING WORDS AND HOMONYMS *QUIZ 1*

Correct all usage errors as listed in Chapter Five. Beware: there may be more than one error per quiz question.

1. It was not just a great day; it was an historic occasion, and I was feeling alright.

2. It takes awhile to adopt to this hot weather when you're from Anchorage.

3. You don't need fancy stationary to thank someone—that's besides the point.

4. I can not be calm on roller coasters. I ride them with baited breath.

5. I have no flare for geography: I thought Buffalo was the capitol of New York, but it's Albany.

6. Where good friends are concerned, my chief criteria has always been loyalty.

7. I prophesized that if she kept acting that way, she'd get her just desserts.

8. You have to be more discrete or you'll literally drive your husband up the wall.

9. I've never waivered in my enjoyment of Shakespeare's plays, i.e., *Romeo and Juliet*.

10. Let's take the next boat off of this island. We'll be in eminent danger if we wait around.

11. I explained my principle reasons for quitting to a couple guys from work.

MORE CONFUSING WORDS AND HOMONYMS *QUIZ 2*

Correct all usage errors as listed in Chapter Five. Beware: there may be more than one error per quiz question.

1. Just wait 'til you see one of the most unique buildings in the Midwest.

2. I always buy Acme products because it's a company who really cares about the consumer.

3. I was amazed by the enormity of his hands, which held me in a vice-like grip.

4. It's not everyday that I get to spend several hours on my favorite past time.

5. He's one of the premiere actors of our generation, irregardless of his messy personal life.

6. It won't phase me in the least if you just sit your drink on the chair next to you.

7. He never graduated high school because he always flaunted the school rules.

8. He wore a gold metal when he lead the parade yesterday.

9. I think it was a fashion misnomer to wear such a miniscule ring with such a big bracelet.

10. Even here in earthquake country, that tremblor was a frightening phenomena.

11. I don't have to show up until 10 A.M. in the morning.

EFFECTIVE WRITING *QUIZ 1*

Rewrite these sentences to make them more effective. Your sentences may be different from the answers given in the book. Answers are in Chapter Seven.

1. While I am in town. Let's visit Golden Gate Park.

2. Walking aimlessly down the street, a bus almost clipped me.

3. Good employees are prompt, courteous, and they help you when you need it.

4. Several items of evidence were overlooked by police who were investigating the scene of the crime.

5. It is expected that you will report for work by no later than nine o'clock.

6. There is just one more thing that I want to say before I finish up.

7. The patient is not unresponsive.

8. Raised in Italy, my grandfather's broken English created problems early on.

9. Students will benefit themselves by listening, taking notes, and they should always pay attention.

10. The cars were worn down by the taxi drivers.

11. After tossing and turning, the alarm came on much too early.

12. I have always believed in being thrifty, loyal, and I do high-quality work.

13. One thing I could say without hesitation is that he is not unreliable.

EFFECTIVE WRITING *QUIZ 2*

Rewrite these sentences to make them more effective. Your sentences may be different from the answers given in the book. Answers are in Chapter Seven.

1. We will utilize the attorneys we have employed to engender the dissolution of our marriage.

2. The boy was hit in the face by the pie as it left the girl's hand.

3. It was not likely that no one would want to claim ownership of the new sports car.

4. We washed the dishes, swept the floor, and the tables were dusted.

5. While singing in the shower, the bar of soap slipped from her hands.

6. Maria encountered a stranger clad in her parka and blue jeans.

7. The weather had adverse impacts on our boat, resulting in the necessity of rescuing us from the water.

8. On a hike with my wife, a bear climbed a tree.

9. Looking back, the dog was following us.

10. Jordan did not believe that Serena had embarrassed him unintentionally.

11. Martin could not juggle watching Timmy, making breakfast, and he had a report to write.

12. Like others we questioned, his name was not announced.

13. I was wearing the sweater that Amy knitted at the concert.
14. Lying on a stretcher, they carried him out.

GRAMMAR MASTERY *TEST*

Correct the following sentences. Place a check mark in front of sentences that are correct. Answers are in Chapter Seven.

1. Some of the desserts was left by the end of the birthday party.
2. It was myself and maybe two other people.
3. Dr. Cresta is one of those professors who does whatever it takes to get his point across.
4. Your brilliant excuses almost makes up for your tardiness.
5. Neither Jackson nor Jenna is playing hooky.
6. Neither Jackson nor his family are going camping this weekend.
7. Either of us is capable of winning.
8. All of the class is willing to take part in the prank.
9. One-third of the eligible population tend not to vote in national elections.
10. Not even one-third of the voters tends to cast their ballots in national elections.
11. Here's the paper clips you requested.
12. She is one of those doctors who make house calls.
13. Her and him are always fighting.
14. When Toni and him come over, we always have a great time.
15. It is we who must decide whether to tax ourselves or cut spending.
16. Between you and I, this class is a joke.
17. Whom do you think you are to give me advice about dating?
18. Who makes up these English rules anyway?
19. Whom do you think should win?
20. Who are you voting for?
21. She is one of the only teachers who does what it takes to help her students learn joyfully.
22. Whomever has the keys gets to be in the driver's seat.
23. We are willing to work with whoever you recommend.
24. The thoughts that Ted presented at the meeting were worthwhile.
25. The thoughts that Ted presented, that were about shifting national priorities, were well received.

26. When you do a job so good, you can expect a raise.

27. I, as most people, try to be considerate of others.

28. Harry smells good. What is the aftershave he is wearing?

29. Lisa did so well on the test that she was allowed to accelerate to the next level.

30. Our puppy is the least hungriest of the litter.

31. He's a man whom I think defines greatness.

32. Karen should of known that her cheap umbrella would break in the storm.

33. Sometimes the effects of our generosity may seem minimal, but our good intentions do make a difference.

34. Ben thought he had lain my jacket on that bench.

35. Our company policy will not allow me to except a gift worth more than $50.

36. They thought we were late, but my wife and I were all ready at the restaurant.

37. Irregardless of who was there first, we were all very hungry and ready to eat.

38. We could hardly believe the Giants could loose the game by that many runs.

39. Isn't it amazing how long that mime can remain completely stationery?

40. The department's principal concern is the safety of all employees.

41. How did they manage to serve cold ice cream in the middle of the vast dessert?

42. The boss complemented Ari on his excellent presentation.

43. The judge did not believe any of there stories.

44. Ilana said she wanted to become a FBI agent when she grew up.

45. It's not good when your always late like this.

46. To be a good billiards player, you've got to think farther ahead than just the next shot.

47. I think I'll go lay down awhile.

48. The golf course at the resort is lovely, but I prefer it's swimming pool.

49. Sam and myself paid the cab fare, and Alejandro paid for dinner.

50. Marta completed five less problems than I did in the same amount of time.

PUNCTUATION, CAPITALIZATION, AND WRITING NUMBERS *PRETEST*

Correct any errors in punctuation, capitalization, and writing numbers. Place a check mark in front of sentences that are correct. Answers are in Chapter Seven.

1. Go West three blocks and turn right.

2. He insisted it was based on the peoples' right to know.

3. "How," I asked "Can you always be so forgetful"?

4. I want you to meet my best friend Bill when he gets here.

5. Although we have a competent staff; bottlenecks do occur.

6. I did not receive the order; therefore, I will not pay my bill.

7. We offer a variety of drinks, for instance beer and wine.

8. Is that book your's?

9. We have much to do, for example, the carpets need vacuuming.

10. Estimates for the work have been forwarded, and a breakdown of costs has been included.

11. Because of his embezzling the company went bankrupt.

12. A proposal that makes harassment of whales illegal, has just passed.

13. He is the President of our corporation.

14. Paolo hurried to the depot to meet his aunt, and two cousins.

15. Finish your job, it is imperative that you do.

16. Sofia and Aidan's house was recently painted.

17. "Stop it!" I said, "Don't ever do that again."

18. He was born in Ames, Iowa and still lives there.

19. "Would you like to accompany me," he asked?

20. I have always had a mental block against Math.

21. He is a strong healthy man.

22. To apply for this job you must have previous experience.

23. Marge, the woman with blond hair will be our speaker this evening.

24. He thought quickly, and then answered the question in complete detail.

25. He asked if he could be excused?

26. It is hailing; not raining.

27. We will grant you immunity, if you decide to cooperate with us.

28. You signed the contract, consequently you must provide us with the raw materials.

29. I would like; however, to read the fine print first.

30. You are required to bring the following: Sleeping bag, food, and a sewing kit.

31. The three company's computers were stolen.

32. The womens' department is upstairs and to your left.

33. It hurt it's paw.

34. One of the lawyer's left her briefcase.

35. That's the Texas' way of doing things.

36. July 5, 1990 was the day I was born.

37. I need to locate four states on the map; Arkansas, Ohio, Illinois, and Utah.

38. The e-mail read, "Hi Camille. I haven't heard from you in two weeks."

39. The veterinarian said, "Unless its bleeding and doesn't stop, don't worry about it."

40. Not wanting to discuss this with her mother anymore, Wendy declared, "This is her karma not mine."

41. You must study hard, to get good grades at a major university.

42. $\frac{1}{4}$ of the police force voted for a pay raise.

43. Thirty one people were injured.

44. I owe you $15.00, not $16.

COMMAS AND PERIODS *QUIZ 1*

Correct any comma or period errors. Place a check mark in front of sentences that are correct. Answers are in Chapter Seven.

1. Ophelia is picking up the food and I am making the centerpieces.

2. "Yes," Ting said "I did see the baby panda at the zoo today."

3. Her mother is planning a trip to Portland, Maine in the fall this year.

4. Patrick's name was on the guest list, wasn't it?

5. Yes, Mother I did remember to place the bakery order.

6. Jackson's white cat was born in June, 2013, at his farm.

7. Jackson's white cat was born on June 28 2013 at his farm.

8. You may only bring the bare essentials to the exam, i.e. a watch, a pencil or a pen, paper, and a calculator.

9. Pencils, pens, paper, calculators, etc., will be provided.

10. I would be hesitant however, to take the trip alone.

11. He hosted a cowboy-themed party in the big, red barn.

12. It looks like A.J. Jefferson, Jr. will be our next congressman.

13. If you are interested in working for our company send us your résumé.

14. My oldest cousin who lives in Detroit used to be a policeman.

15. Jonathan Green M.D. will be the keynote speaker at the conference.

16. The keynote speaker at the conference will be Jonathan Green, M.D..

17. Well do you think we'll see the sun today?

18. Frank visited the travel agent, but still did not book his trip.

19. I want to go now not later.

20. I really enjoyed the show, the acting was superb.

COMMAS AND PERIODS *QUIZ 2*

Correct any comma or period errors. Place a check mark in front of sentences that are correct. Answers are in Chapter Seven.

1. I took Angie the one with the freckles to the movie last night.

2. Jeremy, and I, have had our share of arguments.

3. You are I am sure, telling the truth.

4. She left Albany, New York on January 18 of that year.

5. I need sugar, butter, and eggs, from the grocery store.

6. Dairy products, e.g. milk, butter, eggs, etc. are no longer foods I can eat.

7. Please Sasha, come home as soon as you can.

8. Although you may be right I cannot take your word for it.

9. If you decide to cooperate with us we will grant you immunity.

10. I am typing a letter and she is talking on the phone.

11. She finished her work, and then took a long lunch.

12. Mae said "Why don't you come up and see me sometime?"

13. You said that I could go, didn't you?

14. To apply for this job you must have a Social Security card.

15. He seems to be such a lonely quiet man doesn't he?

16. She wore a bright red dress.

17. She has a good healthy attitude about her work.

18. On June 7, 2012 Hector earned his computer science degree.

19. I like anchovies on my pizza my wife hates them.

20. Although my wife hates anchovies. I like them on my pizza.

SEMICOLONS AND COLONS *QUIZ 1*

Correct any punctuation errors. Some sentences may require removing punctuation. Place a check mark in front of sentences that are correct. Answers are in Chapter Seven.

Example: *These are some of the pool rules; do not run, report unsafe behavior to the lifeguard, and have fun.*

Correction: *These are some of the pool rules: do not run, report unsafe behavior to the lifeguard, and have fun.*

1. Denise prefers to eat chicken or fish: I'm a vegetarian.

2. The centerpieces had her favorite flowers; roses, carnations, and daisies.

3. They were missing a few things on their camping trip, namely; they forgot sunscreen, towels, and firewood.

4. Please give me some time, I do not want to be rushed.

5. While visiting the beach, we saw: pelicans, stingrays, and iguanas.

6. I would like to leave early in the morning, therefore: I am going to bed soon.

7. On our last trip we stayed in Nashville, Tennessee, Atlanta, Georgia, and Orlando, Florida.

8. The girls on the team will have quite a few expenses; uniforms; shoes; equipment; and camp fees.

9. Estella landed her dream summer job: She'll be an intern in a senator's office.

10. Roberto can't decide among three careers: dentist; veterinarian; or physical therapist.

11. When Jane leaves, which will be in a few minutes, we can plan her party, but we still better do it quietly.

12. The players have only one goal, they want to win the Stanley Cup.

13. I need to buy: shampoo, toothpaste, soap, and contact lens solution.

14. Give her a break, she just started working here two days ago!

15. The delegates came from our offices in Region 1, Boston, Region 2, New York, Region 6, Houston, and Region 10, Seattle.

16. Her new supervisor gave her a list of rules to be followed at the office; no making personal phone calls, surfing the Internet, or reading magazines.

17. Jobs were assigned to the shelter volunteers; clean the litter boxes, sweep the floors, feed the cats, and give them water.

18. Max and Sue have been to the Caribbean many times, however; they have not visited St. Lucia.

19. At the camp the children were divided into two groups; those who know how to swim; and those who do not.

20. Ashley was late for the rehearsal: she is usually late.

SEMICOLONS AND COLONS *QUIZ 2*

Correct any punctuation errors. Some sentences may require removing punctuation. Place a check mark in front of sentences that are correct. Answers are in Chapter Seven.

> *Example*:   *We told Annika that we would take three courses next fall; French,*
> *American literature, and advanced algebra.*
>
> *Correction*:   *We told Annika that we would take three courses next fall: French,*
> *American literature, and advanced algebra.*

1. You asked for forgiveness, he granted it to you.

2. We ask therefore, that you keep this matter confidential.

3. The order was requested six weeks ago, therefore I expected the shipment to have arrived by now.

4. The American flag has three colors, namely, red, white, and blue.

5. Clothes are often made from synthetic material; for instance, rayon.

6. If you believe in magic, magical things will happen, but if you don't believe in magic, you'll discover nothing magical.

7. The orchestra, excluding the violin section was not up to par.

8. I have been to San Francisco, California, Reno, Nevada, and Seattle, Washington.

9. I need a few items at the store; clothespins, a bottle opener, and napkins.

10. I answered the phone, no one seemed to be on the other end of the line.

11. I wanted a cup of coffee, not a glass of milk.

12. We have set this restriction, do your homework before watching television.

13. If you can possibly arrange it, please visit us but if you cannot, let us know.

14. I gave her a lot of money while we were married therefore I do not wish to pay her a dime in alimony.

15. We have a variety of desserts, for instance apple pie, chocolate mousse, and flan.

16. I needed three cards to win the hand, namely the ten of hearts, jack of diamonds, and king of hearts.

17. I needed three cards to win the hand; the ten of hearts, jack of diamonds, and king of hearts.

18. I would, therefore like to have an explanation for the missing cash.

19. Nature lovers will appreciate seeing: whales, sea lions, and pelicans.

20. He has friends from Iowa and Nebraska and Illinois is his home state.

QUESTION MARKS AND QUOTATION MARKS *QUIZ 1*

Correct the punctuation errors in the following sentences. Place a check mark in front of sentences that are correct. Answers are in Chapter Seven.

> ***Example***:   *"Well, I really don't know" she said.*
> ***Correction***:   *"Well, I really don't know," she said.*

1. "Have you already completed our survey," the cashier asked?

2. Yan inquired, "Is it supposed to snow tomorrow"?

3. I wonder why Allen left so early this morning?

4. "Are we really planning to drive straight through without stopping," he asked in amazement?

5. I hope you don't mind my asking she said, "but do you realize how tired everyone is going to be by the time we get there"?

6. Shia asked, with disbelief "Are you sure you want to be the one to tell her?"

7. Betty is the one who found out first, isn't she.

8. "Victor asked me what I did yesterday?" she said.

9. She said, "T.J. shouted, "We are not staying at that hotel."

10. Carmella wanted to know if you need a ride to the mall.

QUESTION MARKS AND QUOTATION MARKS *QUIZ 2*

Correct the punctuation errors in the following sentences. Place a check mark in front of sentences that are correct. Answers are in Chapter Seven.

> **Example**:   *He asked, "Did Danika really say that"?*
> **Correction**:   *He asked, "Did Danika really say that?"*

1. He wanted to know when you will be here?

2. "Well, she said, "you certainly didn't waste any time."

3. "Is it almost over," he asked?

4. "I've had it up to here!", she screamed.

5. The song asks, "Would you like to swing on a star"?

6. Carmen said, "She vowed, "I'll never leave you."

7. "May I have a rain check on that lunch"? I asked.

8. Do you believe the saying, "It is better to vote for what you want and not get it than to vote for what you don't want and get it?"

9. Bernard said, Waldo asked, "Who took my pencil sharpener?"

10. "May I see your ID card," the clerk asked?

PARENTHESES AND BRACKETS *QUIZ 1*

Correct the punctuation errors in the following sentences. Place a check mark in front of sentences that are correct. Answers are in Chapter Seven.

1. After standing in line for 30 minutes [or possibly longer], she was able to buy the tickets.

2. My cousin wrote, "I herd (*sic*) a rumor that Jack and Jennifer are getting engaged."

3. I would like to confirm my membership (The dues check is enclosed.)

4. Our first meeting will be held at First Central Bank's community room [Main Street branch].

5. We all decided to go out for pizza after the meeting (except for Dan).

6. I overheard her say, "Our favorite cousin (she meant Dale) will be accompanying us on our trip."

7. Yasir was able to find the book he wanted for a really good price (twenty-five dollars.)

8. Luigi moved to this country shortly after he was born (about 1925).

9. When his family came to the United States, they settled in Washington [state].

10. The first line of his letter said, "My freinds [sic], I never thought we would all be together again like this."

PARENTHESES AND BRACKETS *QUIZ 2*

Correct the punctuation errors in the following sentences. Place a check mark in front of sentences that are correct. Answers are in Chapter Seven.

1. She requested (actually she pleaded, that her name be withheld.

2. Joe called today (He's been sick.) and said he felt better.

3. I can have lunch with you tomorrow (Friday.)

4. I hope you are feeling better (I am sick today.)

5. In the movie Vanessa exclaims, "Whatever shall I do if he (the sheriff) comes looking for you tomorrow?"

6. I read in the Mill Valley police log: "Officers were called to disburse (sic) attendees at a noisy party."

7. Daniel wanted to know why Mindy felt that way (he really didn't understand it.).

8. Mariella told us that when her grandfather was a child, he used to work at a hamburger stand for almost nothing [sixty-five cents an hour].

9. I need to run to the store right away (it's going to close in 20 minutes.)

10. "do not go to sleep angry at each other," the author states on page 56.

APOSTROPHES *QUIZ 1*

Correct any apostrophe errors. Answers are in Chapter Seven.

1. The movie had it's desired effect.

2. Both of my brother-in-law's live near Durango.

3. Those girl's vitality and humor are infectious.

4. *Womens' Wear Daily* has been called the industry's voice of authority.

5. Those actress's costumes look beautiful on them.

6. Bill and Al had a boat. I was there when Bill's and Al's boat sank.

7. She always let me stay up past the other childrens' bedtime.

8. In some peoples' opinion, Faulkner is too difficult.

9. I really felt that I got my monies worth.

10. Would that companies health plan give you peace of mind?

APOSTROPHES *QUIZ 2*

Correct any apostrophe errors. Answers are in Chapter Seven.

1. Those old factory's roof's have all caved in.

2. The two little bird's feather's were ruffled.

3. If it isn't her's, then who's is it?

4. Joe Wilson said, "I may be biased, but the Wilson's holiday meals are the best."

5. Watch out for the scissor's sharp blades.

6. Weve been invited to her two sisters-in-law party.

7. Does'nt it seem strange that I didn't see that friend of your's anywhere?

8. The five injured sailor's relatives are waiting outside.

9. Not all baby's mothers agree on what constitutes good nutrition.

10. Mr. Simms said none of his fellow Simm's opinions would sway him.

HYPHENS BETWEEN WORDS *QUIZ 1*

Add, remove, or fix hyphens as necessary. Place a check mark in front of sentences that are correct. Answers are in Chapter Seven.

1. The storm blew down a seventy foot tall tree last night.

2. The tree that blew down last night was seventy feet tall.

3. My sister is moving from her home next to the heavily-congested highway.

4. The summer camp was designed for 16 year old to 18 year old gymnasts.

5. The summer camp was designed for gymnasts 16 years old to 18 years old.

6. The summer camp was designed for gymnasts 16-18 years old.

7. Clashes came one-year after the prime minister took office.

8. It's a two hour meeting, 2:30 - 4:30 P.M.

9. If we split the bill evenly, we each owe thirty four dollars.

10. We offer around the clock coverage.

11. Those low-interest rates are tempting.

12. He certainly is a slovenly-appearing young man.

HYPHENS BETWEEN WORDS *QUIZ 2*

Add, remove, or fix hyphens as necessary. Place a check mark in front of sentences that are correct. Answers are in Chapter Seven.

1. She jumped from a two story building.

2. You must let-down your guard.

3. You certainly have a go get it nature.

4. The badly-injured fireman was taken to a hospital.

5. Look left-and-right before you cross the street.

6. The left handed pitcher threw fastballs at almost 100 miles per hour.

7. Do you remember anything you read in the fourth grade?

8. This is seventh grade reading material.

9. Beware of high pressure telemarketers.

10. That two year old is adorable.

11. That two-year old child is adorable.

12. That child is two years old.

HYPHENS WITH PREFIXES AND SUFFIXES *QUIZ 1*

Add or remove hyphens as necessary. Place a check mark in front of sentences that are correct. Answers are in Chapter Seven.

1. Construction of the transAlaska oil pipeline had to address issues caused by perma-frost.
2. Our town's exmayor has surprised everyone by deciding to run for reelection.
3. The safety official deemphasized human error as a factor in the accident.
4. Oh no, I've spilled coffee all over myself and will have to redress for dinner.
5. Jacob had to sue the manufacturer to obtain full redress for his injuries.
6. According to Aunt Agnes, half of young people today are semiilliterate.
7. Our farming coop includes a rooster and a coop for five chickens.
8. I suppose hiking twelve miles a day for four days is do-able, but I'd rather not.
9. It is a true-ism that creating a Cubiststyle painting is easier said than done.
10. Would you have guessed that exSenator Salazar would become Governorelect Salazar?

HYPHENS WITH PREFIXES AND SUFFIXES *QUIZ 2*

Insert hyphens or close up the space where appropriate. Answers are in Chapter Seven.

1. non Jewish
2. pre existing
3. re establish
4. self satisfied
5. ex Marine
6. anti inflammatory
7. anti war
8. error free
9. self styled
10. absentee ism

CAPITALIZATION *QUIZ 1*

Correct the following sentences where capitalization errors appear. Place a check mark in front of sentences that are correct. Answers are in Chapter Seven.

1. Don't you love looking at the sky when venus appears next to the Moon?
2. Leslie said that a highlight of her trip to the Nation's Capital was touring the white house.
3. My Grandmother lives on Fillmore street.
4. I will be excited to listen to our Chief Executive Officer, Nancy Williamson, speak today in the auditorium.
5. The new immigration bill has the support of most of our State's Congressional delegation, including senator Mayhew.
6. I plead not guilty, your honor.
7. Have you ever visited New England in the Fall?
8. I told uncle Walter to turn North when he reached Broadway, but he got lost because he's not from Madison county.
9. Uncle Walter said, "please use left or right, not North, South, East, or West."
10. Adriana is dreading Spring Quarter because she has to take Organic Chemistry and Physics 105.
11. Adriana needs to bring the following to her final exam: Two pencils, scratch paper, a calculator, and a light snack.
12. That was amazing how Coach Ernie Sasaki led The Bulldogs to their first winning season.

CAPITALIZATION *QUIZ 2*

Correct the following sentences where capitalization errors appear. Place a check mark in front of sentences that are correct. Answers are in Chapter Seven.

1. She said, "bees are not the only insects that sting."
2. "You must understand," he pleaded, "That I need more time to pay you."
3. Mark Paxton, the Vice President of the company, embezzled over one million dollars.
4. The President of the United States wields much power.

5. I live in the northeastern part of the state, where the climate is colder.

6. The West, especially California, is famous for its cutting-edge technology.

7. Have you read *All The King's Men*?

8. I enjoy Summer more than any other season.

9. Employees of the Company were laid off with little hope of returning to work.

10. The supreme court unanimously struck down the proposed Constitutional Amendment today.

11. We saw Director George Lucas walking down the street.

12. We all stood for the National Anthem before watching The New York Mets play The Chicago Cubs.

WRITING NUMBERS *QUIZ 1*

Correct, simplify, or improve consistency regarding how numbers are expressed in the following sentences. Answers are in Chapter Seven.

1. During the first hours after the plane crash, authorities reported thirty six people missing.

2. 36 people were reported missing during the first hours after the plane crash.

3. The new stadium will hold 43520 fans.

4. Bobby grew .67 inches in three months.

5. Next week's lottery jackpot is expected to reach between four million and 5 million dollars.

6. Next week's lottery jackpot is expected to reach between $4 million dollars and $5 million dollars.

7. The next meeting of the holiday party planning committee will be held on the 31st of October at 12 Noon.

8. The plane won't arrive until 12 P.M.

9. Some people now refer to the Forties and Fifties as "mid-century."

10. Some people now refer to the '40s and '50s as "mid-century."

WRITING NUMBERS *QUIZ 2*

Correct, simplify, or improve consistency regarding how numbers are expressed in the following sentences. Answers are in Chapter Seven.

1. ⅕ of the inventory was ruined in the fire.
2. A two thirds majority is needed to pass the measure.
3. The tree grew only .5 inches because of the drought.
4. Her earnings rose from $500 to $5,000.00 in one year because of her marketing efforts.
5. I paid her all but the last $0.75 today.
6. We all agreed. $2,500 is a lot of money.
7. 47 people were hired last month.
8. Including tax, my new car cost thirty two thousand, six hundred seventy two dollars, fifty seven cents.
9. I will be twenty- one years old on December 9.
10. We have only received point five four inches of rain this year.

PUNCTUATION, CAPITALIZATION, AND WRITING NUMBERS MASTERY *TEST*

Correct any errors in punctuation, capitalization, or writing numbers. Place a check mark in front of sentences that are correct. Answers are in Chapter Seven.

1. I am asking if you would like to roller blade together tomorrow?
2. Yes Jean, you were right about that answer.
3. He said that the book was "In my office if you want to read it", so I took him up on it.
4. Wherever we go people recognize us.
5. Isabel enjoys the museum although she cannot afford the entrance fee.
6. His new book is titled *Food is my Favorite Thing*.
7. You are my friend, however, I cannot afford to lend you any more money.
8. Paul Simon sang, "I am a rock, I am an island."
9. I asked Ella, "Did he want his ring back"?
10. John F. Kennedy, Jr. became a magazine publisher and a pilot before his tragic death.
11. Your house resembles the Johnson's house.
12. The elections will be held on the first Tuesday of November 2008.
13. The elections, will be held on Tuesday, November 4, 2008, and the polls will be kept open until 8:00 P.M.
14. Carl worried about the hurricane but tried to stay calm and help his family.

15. I favor green and yellow and purple is her first choice.

16. I need to locate four states on the map: namely, Minnesota, Michigan, California, and Nevada.

17. This is the point that Einstein made; You cannot fix a problem with the problem.

18. Our Philosophy teacher thinks Einstein meant that we cannot stop war by waging war.

19. Whenever Cheryl is in town she visits her sister.

20. A well reasoned argument was presented for negotiating a peaceful resolution.

21. The argument for negotiating a peaceful resolution was well reasoned.

22. A liberally sprinkled dose of humor was very much appreciated.

23. Our liberal minded clergyman managed to unite the entire congregation.

24. Our clergyman, who united the entire congregation, was liberal-minded.

25. Jan asked, "What did Joe mean when he said, 'I will see you later?' "

26. I asked the Wilson's over for dinner.

27. When I noticed that our dog cut it's paw, I called the veterinarian right away.

28. "Your right to be concerned," said the vet. "I would like to take a look at your dog."

29. Even though its thirty miles to the town where that vet's office is, I wanted to take the drive.

30. The friendly looking vet examined our dog's paw and suggested that we have it bandaged.

31. We had pet insurance but still owed $40 dollars in co-payment fees.

32. Our dog was a semi-invalid until she chewed off the bandage.

33. I guess she did what any self respecting dog would do by grooming herself.

34. The dog has fully re-covered, although I will never be the same.

35. Girls in his family wore hand me down dresses.

36. Wendy thought she knew everything about her mother but found out two years ago that her mother had been married before.

37. When Wendy asked about this marriage, her mother Ilse was hesitant to discuss any details.

38. She will go to her grave with some secrets said Wendy.

39. "Do you understand her need for privacy," Wendy asked her husband?

40. The wealthy became wealthier during the 1990s.

41. The alarm clock went off at 4:00 o'clock.

42. Many people dread the 15 of April in the United States because taxes are due.

43. The check was written for $13348.15.

44. The check was written for three-hundred forty-eight dollars and fifteen cents.

CHAPTER 7

ANSWERS TO QUIZZES

GRAMMAR *PRETEST ANSWERS*

1. How **quickly** he runs.

2. Neither one of them **is** ready yet.

3. The desk and the chair **sit** in the corner.

4. Each of us **was** scheduled to take the test.

5. The coach, not the players, **has** been ill.

6. There **are** only four days until Christmas.

7. She is one of the women who **work** hard.

8. That was Yusuf and **I** whom you saw.

9. This phone call is for Bill and **me**.

10. Terrell is the **smarter** of the two.

11. It was I **who** called.

12. It is **we** clerks who work hard.

13. He took the plate off the table.

14. I am doing fine. How about **you**?

15. They mailed the copies to him and **me**.

16. Neither of the candidates **has** spoken.

17. How will you be **affected** financially if downsizing means you will lose your job?

18. Joan walks **slowly** so her children can keep up with her. (**OR** more slowly)

19. Jake is the **older** of the two brothers.

20. May did **well** on the test she took yesterday.

21. He and she were **really** close friends.

22. **Whoever** drove in the carpool lane without any passengers will be fined.

23. Please allow Jenna or **me** to assist you.

24. It's a company **that** doesn't judge others by their nationalities and accents.

25. They fought over their father's estate because they felt **angry** about the way he had treated them.

26. You look **good** in that running outfit.

27. Don't feel **bad** about forgetting my birthday.

28. We saw two puppies at the pound and took home the **cuter** one.

29. Speak **more clearly** please.

30. Where is that book?

31. Pollen **affects** my sinuses and makes me sneeze.

32. I want to **lie** down for a nap, but the phone keeps ringing.

33. That SUV, **which** landed on its hood after the accident, was traveling at eighty miles per hour.

34. Yesterday, Barry **laid** my jacket on the hood of the car.

35. We need to discuss this **further**.

36. My daughter became **an** honorary member of the city council for the day.

37. The group is on **its** best behavior.

38. **You're** the only one for me.

39. That redwood tree has become taller **than** the oak tree next door.

40. The time for action has long since **passed**.

41. **It's** a long way from here to Tierra del Fuego.

42. Mother, **may** I go to the movies with Ashton this afternoon?

43. I could **have** danced all night.

44. Srdjian **emigrated** from his native Bosnia about five years ago.

45. Did you see the beautiful **brooch** Genevieve was wearing today?

46. The teacher tried to **elicit** a discussion about the novel.

47. La Donna talks fondly about the four years that she went to the university.

48. The answer is **plain** and simple.

49. Let me **set** this book down on the table before I answer your question.

50. The legislature finally authorized the funds to polish the gold on the dome of the **capitol** building.

FINDING NOUNS, VERBS, AND SUBJECTS *QUIZ 1 ANSWERS*

1. The overturned <u>truck</u> <u>blocked</u> both lanes.

2. <u>He</u> <u>appears</u> to be deep in thought.

3. The <u>Metropolitan Museum of Art</u> <u>is</u> a New York City landmark.

4. <u>She</u> <u>will fly</u> part of the way and then <u>drive</u> fifty kilometers to get there.

5. <u>Honesty</u> <u>is</u> the best policy.

6. (<u>You</u>) <u>Get</u> over here quickly!

7. From the bottom of the cave, the <u>stalagmites</u> <u>rose</u> ten feet high.

8. Through the mist, the **<u>bridge</u>** <u>appeared</u>.

9. <u>I</u> <u>will</u> just <u>be watching</u> the **B**oston **M**arathon, but my <u>wife</u> <u>will be running</u> in it.

10. Behind the door <u>is</u> a coat <u>rack</u>.

11. <u>Joe</u> <u>has been helping out</u> with the chores.

12. <u>He</u> <u>should have been</u> more gracious.

FINDING NOUNS, VERBS, AND SUBJECTS *QUIZ 2 ANSWERS*

1. <u>He</u> <u>depends</u> on her in times of need.

2. (<u>You</u>) <u>Watch</u> your step.

3. The insurance **<u>agent</u>** <u>gave</u> her sound advice.

4. On the table <u>was</u> her <u>purse</u>.

5. In the newspaper, an interesting <u>article</u> <u>appeared</u>.

6. (<u>You</u>) <u>Look</u> before <u>you</u> <u>leap</u>.

7. Across the road <u>lived</u> her <u>boyfriend</u>.

8. <u>We</u> <u>are forced</u> to inhale and exhale this smog-filled air. (**OR** <u>are</u>)

9. <u>I</u> <u>found</u> a shiny new dime in the gutter.

10. Around every cloud <u>is</u> a silver <u>lining</u>.

11. How long <u>have</u> <u>you</u> <u>been living</u> in **N**ew Delhi?

12. <u>They</u> <u>must have given up</u> eventually.

SUBJECT AND VERB AGREEMENT *QUIZ 1 ANSWERS*

1. That <u>pack</u> of lies <u>is</u> not <u>going</u> to cause me to change my mind.

2. My favorite team's <u>colors</u> <u>are</u> orange and black. (CORRECT)

3. Here <u>are</u> two more <u>factors</u> to consider.

4. Neither the <u>rain</u> nor the <u>darkness</u> <u>is going</u> to stop me.

5. My <u>staff</u> <u>believes</u> in providing high-quality service. (CORRECT)

6. <u>This</u> <u>is</u> one of the <u>things</u> that <u>bother</u> me about grammar.

7. <u>Mary Lou</u> <u>asked</u> that <u>he</u> <u>take out</u> the trash. (CORRECT)

8. Either the <u>bikes</u> or the <u>lawn mower</u> <u>goes</u> in that space.

9. Oh my, there <u>are</u> not enough <u>desserts</u> for everyone.

10. The <u>bag</u> of toys <u>is going</u> to a needy family. (CORRECT)

11. Neither my <u>brother</u> nor my <u>sister-in-law</u> <u>is taking</u> Mom to the doctor.

12. The <u>conductor</u>, as well as the musicians, <u>is taking</u> the stage.

13. A <u>majority</u> of the community <u>supports</u> lower speed limits.

14. My whole <u>family</u> <u>is vacationing</u> in Baja California this winter.

15. <u>Did</u> <u>he</u> <u>say</u> sixty dollars <u>is</u> the cost of going to the ball game?

16. The <u>distance</u> alone, besides the costs involved, <u>is</u> too great to consider moving.

17. <u>Law and order</u> <u>is</u> the principle <u>he</u> <u>based</u> his campaign on. (CORRECT)

18. There<u>'s</u> <u>lots</u> of food left. (CORRECT; the verb is -'s, a contraction of *is*.)

19. There <u>are</u> <u>lots</u> of people here.

20. If <u>it</u> <u>were</u> up to me, <u>we</u> <u>would leave</u> earlier in the morning.

21. <u>One</u> in three stressed Americans <u>copes</u> by shopping.

22. <u>Four years</u> <u>is</u> considered the normal amount of time to earn a bachelor's degree.

SUBJECT AND VERB AGREEMENT *QUIZ 2 ANSWERS*

1. <u>Al</u> and <u>Eli</u> <u>go</u> to the beach to surf with their friends. (CORRECT)

2. There <u>are</u> three <u>strawberries</u> left.

3. The <u>group</u> of children from that school <u>has</u> never <u>seen</u> the ocean. (CORRECT)

4. If our staff <u>members</u> <u>keep picking</u> at each other, <u>we</u> <u>will</u> not <u>meet</u> our goals. (CORRECT)

5. A <u>lot</u> of things <u>she</u> <u>said</u> <u>were</u> the truth.

6. My <u>problem</u>, <u>which</u> <u>is</u> minor in comparison with others, <u>exists</u> because <u>I</u> <u>dropped out</u> of high school.

7. <u>Most</u> of my savings <u>are invested</u> in real estate.

8. <u>She's</u> one of those professionals <u>who</u> really <u>pay</u> attention.

9. <u>Some</u> of my goals <u>have</u> yet to be met.

10. <u>All</u> of my goals <u>are being met</u> and <u>surpassed</u>. (CORRECT)

11. <u>None</u> of this <u>is</u> your business. (CORRECT)

12. <u>Nervousness</u>, not to mention lack of sleep, <u>contributes</u> to poor performance.

13. <u>One-third</u> of the city <u>is experiencing</u> a blackout tonight.

14. <u>One-third</u> of the people <u>are suffering</u>. (CORRECT)

15. The next <u>thing</u> I <u>heard</u> <u>was</u> two shots.

16. Ladies and gentlemen, here <u>are</u> <u>Wisin</u> and <u>Yandel</u>.

17. Neither <u>Darren</u> nor <u>Ida</u> <u>is</u> capable of such a crime.

18. <u>Eighty miles</u> on one charge <u>is</u> the maximum range for my electric car.

19. <u>I</u> <u>wish</u> <u>it</u> <u>were</u> summer and time for vacation. (CORRECT)

20. Her <u>attitude</u> <u>is</u> one of the <u>things</u> that <u>are</u> different.

PRONOUNS *QUIZ 1 ANSWERS*

1. It is **he** who will be responsible for making all of the arrangements.

2. It is I who **am** wrong.

3. I hope my boss gives that assignment to Laura and **me**.

4. She was one of those cruise passengers who **are** always complaining.

5. Each of the players **gets** to make a speech before the parade.

6. Julia is a faster runner than **I**.

7. The sweater that we found at the church is **yours**.

8. The dog hurt **its** paw while running through the empty field.

9. George and **I** finished staining the deck.

10. Everyone wrote **his or her** own autobiography in the class.

11. **She** and Carlos are the baby's godparents.

12. The honors committee nominated **him** and Ming.

13. Everyone working on this together **has** come to **a different conclusion**.

14. You more than anyone else **know** what the risks are.

15. **She** and **I** are in charge of the sales presentation tomorrow.

16. Neither of the girls **is** planning a wedding in the near future.

17. It is **we** who will get the blame if things do not go well.

18. **It's** obvious that the best team will prevail.

19. Nora is one of the candidates who **are** worthy of my vote.

20. Nora, of all the candidates who **are** running, is the best.

PRONOUNS *QUIZ 2 ANSWERS*

1. Meagan said she looked forward to seeing **him** and **me** at the airport.

2. **He** and **I** have been good friends since second grade.

3. Yes, this is **she** speaking.

4. My friend, unlike **me**, is very artistic.

5. Please talk to Daniela or **me** next time you have a concern.

6. As I've said before, ask either Boris or **her**, not me.

7. None of the doctors have been able to figure out what is wrong with **her** or **me**.

8. She is as stubborn as **he**, but that's no surprise given they are sister and brother.

9. I weigh more than **he does. OR** I weigh more than **he**.

10. **Whose** hat is this?

11. It is **we** who **deserve** credit for this company's third-quarter profits.

12. **It's** a shame that some of the profits have been wasted on excessive executive compensation packages.

13. If you have any questions, please call either Randy or **me**.

14. **My friend** and **I** will stop by on our way to the bakery. (This format is preferred over *I and my friend will stop by on our way to the bakery.*)

15. You can help him or me but probably not both of us. (CORRECT)

16. It is **I** who **am** to blame.

17. My boss and **I** will pick up where the others left off.

18. When the horse kicked **its** legs, the rider landed in the lake.

19. **Your** friend told **her friend** to tell my friend that **there's** a party tonight.

20. The argument he gave had **its** merits.

WHO, WHOM, WHOEVER, WHOMEVER *QUIZ 1 ANSWERS*

1. **Who** brought the mail in today?

2. He is the doctor **who** took Jimmy's tonsils out.

3. **Whom** did you go to the movie with?

4. There will be a prize awarded to **whoever** finishes first.

5. Fatima was the cashier **who** won the lottery.

6. It does not matter to me **who** drives tomorrow.

7. I will be happy to help **whoever** needs extra assistance.

8. Sheila will have her hair styled by **whomever** her friend Rhonda recommends.

9. I will ride with **whoever** is planning to stop at the store.

10. **Whoever** wrote the story did an excellent job.

11. Next week they will decide **who** will be on the varsity team.

12. Please thank **whoever** brought in our mail while we were gone.

13. Andre is the person **who** we think is the most qualified.

14. We will hire **whomever** you trust to do the work.

15. **Whoever** used the grill last forgot to clean it.

16. **Whom** are you mailing that letter to?

17. I will drive **whomever** Orlando decides to invite to the game.

18. **Whom** do you trust to fix your computer?

19. **Whoever** can eat 25 hot wings will win a T-shirt.

20. The wedding florist **whom** we wanted to hire is unavailable.

WHO, WHOM, WHOEVER, WHOMEVER *QUIZ 2 ANSWERS*

1. **Who** is your closest friend?

2. **Whom** do you bank with?

3. **Who** do you think will win the award?

4. Clare knows **who** the winner is already.

5. Omar will talk about his girlfriend with **whoever** asks him.

6. Kimiko donates her time to **whoever** she feels needs it most.

7. Quinton will work on the project with **whomever** you suggest.

8. **Who** was that in the clown costume?

9. Kathy was not sure **whom** she was voting for.

10. **Whoever** wins the lottery will become a millionaire.

11. He is the man **whom** Mr. O'Brian hired.

12. She is the woman **who** I believe was hired last year.

13. **Whom** were you speaking about just now?

14. **Who** do you think will do the work best?

15. I will vote for **whoever** you think is best.

16. I will vote for **whomever** you suggest.

17. **Whom** shall I ask about this matter?

18. Give the information to **whoever** requests it.

19. Give the information to **whomever** they prefer.

20. **Who** do you suppose runs this show?

WHO, WHOM, THAT, WHICH *QUIZ 1 ANSWERS*

1. Tina is looking for a pet **that** is small and easy to care for.

2. Andre was the boy **whom** we hired to shovel our snow.

3. The package **that** was left on the porch was our book order.

4. The mechanic **that** fixed my car did a great job. (CORRECT) **OR** The mechanic **who** fixed my car did a great job.

5. I hope we can find a restaurant **that** we can all agree on. (CORRECT)

6. The red vase, **which** she sold for $20, was worth $200.

7. Mike is having a difficult time finding a tutor **whom** we can afford.

8. That is the mascara **which** caused my allergic reaction. ("That is the mascara *that* caused my allergic reaction" is not incorrect. However, when *that* has already appeared in a sentence, writers sometimes use *which* to avoid awkward formations.)

9. Was he the only student in the class **who** applied for the scholarship? (CORRECT)

10. My favorite store, **which** is closing Friday, is having a big sale. (CORRECT)

WHO, WHOM, THAT, WHICH *QUIZ 2 ANSWERS*

1. Ahmed is the skydiver **that** broke his back last week. (CORRECT) **OR** Ahmed is the skydiver **who** broke his back last week.

2. That **which** doesn't kill you makes you stronger.

3. I love hearing the owls **that** sit in the trees and hoot at dusk.

4. The domino theory, **which** stated that when one country fell to communism, others in the area would be likely to fall, was used as an argument to continue the Vietnam War.

5. The game **that** intrigues Gretchen the most is dominoes.

6. Gandhi was a role model **whom** millions admired.

7. The tomatoes **that** grow in her garden are unlike those you buy in a store.

8. The tomatoes from her garden, **which** grew larger than those in the grocery store, were sweet and ripe. (CORRECT)

9. The baker **whom** we hired should win an award.

ADJECTIVES AND ADVERBS *QUIZ 1 ANSWERS*

1. Allison runs very **clumsily**.

2. Her boyfriend said she looked **good** in her new dress. (CORRECT)

3. I feel just as **bad** about this as you do.

4. I did **well** today on my final exam.

5. C.J. slept **soundly** after running the marathon.

6. Despite her honest efforts, my grandmother's driving is **worse** than ever.

7. To dance **well**, you have to practice a lot.

8. Of your three dogs, which is **cutest**?

9. School policy says that children should stay home from school if they do not feel **well**. (CORRECT)

10. Your house looks **similar** to the Johnsons' house.

11. Eat **more daintily** please.

12. Do you like soccer or basketball **better**?

13. You should speak **more carefully** around my daughter.

14. He still hears **well** for someone who's played in a rock band for twenty years.

15. His hearing is **good** for someone who's played in a rock band for twenty years. (CORRECT)

16. Our homemade fried rice was **really** tasty.

17. I think my left eye is my **sharper** eye.

18. Dana did not get into her favorite college because her essay was written **badly**.

19. He looked **pensive** sitting cross-legged under the willow tree. (CORRECT)

20. These days, children don't know how to treat each other **nicely**.

ADJECTIVES AND ADVERBS *QUIZ 2 ANSWERS*

1. Come **quickly** or we will miss our bus.

2. He swings the bat as **well** as anyone in major-league baseball.

3. I have never been **less sure** of anything in my life.

4. Ella was the **better** of the two sisters at gymnastics.

5. You did that somersault so **well**.

6. Rochelle felt **bad** about forgetting Devlin's birthday.

7. This is the **worst** oil spill I have ever seen. (CORRECT)

8. The jasmine has bloomed and smells very **sweet**. (CORRECT)

9. She looked **suspicious** to the man wearing the trench coat.

10. She looked **suspiciously** at the man wearing the trench coat. (CORRECT)

11. To find her, we need to follow **this** set of tracks. (**OR that**)

12. Who is the **fastest** runner: Usain, Johan, or Justin?

13. Do you feel **happy** about your performance on the math quiz?

14. The new model of this chain saw operates much **more quietly** than the old model.

15. She felt **good** about getting her puppy from the SPCA. (CORRECT)

16. You'd better be able to prove that, of all the candidates, you're **most** qualified.

17. Which is **worse**, a toothache or a headache?

18. She reacted **swiftly**, which made him feel **bad** about insulting her.

19. The herbs in the salad tasted **bitter**. (CORRECT)

20. Sharon fought **bitterly** against her ex-husband for custody of their daughter. (CORRECT)

PREPOSITIONS *QUIZ 1 ANSWERS*

1. We could **have** been there by now if we hadn't gotten lost.

2. Where did you buy that beautiful necklace?

3. Charles talks **the way** his brother does.

4. He drove his car **into** the garage.

5. Did you take an envelope off my desk?

6. Where did Nadia's little dog go?

7. **As** the ranger said, this is an area with a lot of poison ivy.

8. Stacey's copy of the book was different **from** mine.

9. Jacques acted **as if** he never met your aunt.

10. The tour guide led our group into the library. (CORRECT)

PREPOSITIONS *QUIZ 2 ANSWERS*

1. Where did you get this?

2. I could **have** danced all night.

3. This problem is no different **from** many others I've dealt with.

4. The lioness ate **as if** she hadn't eaten food in a week. (**OR as though**)

5. Take your plate off the table.

6. Cut the pie into six slices.

7. I don't know what you are talking about. (CORRECT)

8. You could **have** told me about the mistake earlier.

9. I don't know where he is, or I would tell you.

10. I'm going to turn this lost wallet **in to** the police.

AFFECT VS. EFFECT *QUIZ 1 ANSWERS*

1. Mark told Taneisha that cigarettes would negatively **affect** her health.

2. The service trip to Central America had a life-altering **effect** on Rosemary.

3. To **effect** better treatment of food-packaging laborers, Aaron started a workers union.

4. The convict showed little **affect** throughout her trial.

5. When the school's new rules take **effect**, students will no longer be allowed to leave campus during lunch.

6. Do you think our campaign will be **effective**?

7. Bobby's friends tend to **affect** his rash decision making.

8. Working overtime at the office negatively **affected** Keeton's personal life.

9. It is unfortunate that fossil fuels have such a drastic **effect** on the environment.

10. One must be a powerful speaker to **effect** social change.

11. Jojo found that meditation had therapeutic **effects**.

12. The choices we make now will **affect** society for generations to come.

13. Professor Nguyen's harsh grading had the unintended **effect** of discouraging interest in the course.

14. The bike safety law currently in **effect** should be improved.

15. The emergence of social networking websites **affected** her productivity.

16. Do you think that winning the lottery has **affected** Jujhaar's personality?

AFFECT VS. EFFECT *QUIZ 2 ANSWERS*

1. The **effect** of the antibiotic on her infection was surprising.

2. I did not know that antibiotics could **affect** people so quickly.

3. Plastic surgery had an **effect** not only on her appearance but also on her self-esteem.

4. If the chemotherapy has no **effect**, should she get surgery for the tumor?

5. When will we know if the chemotherapy has taken **effect**?

6. Losing her hair from chemotherapy did not **affect** her as much as her friends had expected.

7. To have the most **effect**, you should know both your strengths and your weaknesses.

8. The movie *Winged Migration* had two **effects** on him: he became an environmental advocate and a bird lover.

9. The net **effect** of blowing the whistle on her boss was that she was eventually given his position.

10. What was the **effect** of his promotion?

11. His decision **affected** everyone here.

12. We had to **effect** a reduction in costs.

13. The critics greatly **affected** his thinking.

14. How were you able to **effect** such radical changes?

15. That book had a major **effect** on his philosophy.

LAY VS. LIE *QUIZ 1 ANSWERS*

1. Grandma is not feeling well and went to **lie** down.

2. The mail has **lain** on the table unopened for two days now.

3. The cat will probably be **lying** in the sun after she eats her lunch. (CORRECT)

4. The chickens **laid** enough eggs for us to make three large omelets.

5. Bobby has been **laying** his clothes on the bed instead of folding them.

6. The girls **lay** in the tent and pretended they were camping out.

7. Omar **lay** on the air mattress and floated on the water for hours.

8. He forgot where he had **laid** his keys.

9. **Lay** out all the clothes that you want to pack. (CORRECT)

10. You should have **laid** out all the clothes that you wanted to pack.

LAY VS. LIE *QUIZ 2 ANSWERS*

1. I am dizzy and need to **lie** down.

2. When I got dizzy yesterday, I **lay** down.

3. My brother **lays** carpet for a living. (CORRECT)

4. That rug has **lain** there for decades. (CORRECT)

5. We need to **lay** this baby down for a nap.

6. We will know we have **laid** this issue to rest when we no longer fight about it.

7. The lions are **lying** in wait for their prey.

8. The lions have **lain** in wait for their prey.

9. I **laid** the blanket over her as she slept. (CORRECT)

10. I will **lay** my head on my pillow.

ADVICE VS. ADVISE *QUIZ 1 ANSWERS*

1. My doctor **advised** me to go to the gym more often.

2. I always ask my brother for **advice** because he knows me best.

3. My **advice** is to talk to Georgia face-to-face, rather than by e-mail.

4. The traffic reporters **advise** commuters to take the back roads because of the accident on the freeway.

5. If you are interested in becoming a marine biologist, I would **advise** you to talk to Hank.

6. Even though Scott always gives Eden bad **advice**, she still follows it.

7. Although Bhaven is not very opinionated, he gives astute **advice**.

8. Teachers **advise** parents to emphasize reading at home.

9. When giving **advice** to a friend, I try to put myself in her shoes.

10. The ride operator **advises** passengers to keep their limbs inside the roller coaster.

ADVICE VS. ADVISE *QUIZ 2 ANSWERS*

1. Adele is always happy to offer **advice** if you ask her for it.

2. The lawyer **advised** him to plead guilty.

3. If you want to go on the senior trip, I would strongly **advise** you to start saving your money.

4. Our new members are impressed with the level of **advice** they received from the leadership group.

5. Sara always takes my **advice** to heart.

6. I'd like to ask an engineer to **advise** us on the design.

7. We **advised** the city council that the deadline was tentative and might need to be extended.

8. Lakeisha knows she can always go to her best friend for **advice**.

9. Don't give **advice** that you're not willing to follow yourself.

10. Randall has a bad habit of offering unsolicited **advice**.

THEIR VS. THERE VS. THEY'RE *QUIZ 1 ANSWERS*

1. The Garcias are having a costume party at **their** house tonight.

2. I heard that the best beaches are in Southern California, but I would rather not drive all the way down **there**.

3. While **they're** in town, we want to show LaDasha and Raquel the beach at sunset.

4. **There** are many ways to cut a cake.

5. Celia allows her children to watch television once they have finished **their** homework.

6. Paul and Summer are in search of a tank for **their** baby turtles.

7. On Thursday, **they're** going to take a paragliding lesson.

8. After a long day of work, **their** brains were fried.

9. Even though **there** is not enough space in my room for that tree, my dad refuses to move it.

10. To our surprise, Nick and Taylor just announced that **they're** getting married!

THEIR VS. THERE VS. THEY'RE *QUIZ 2 ANSWERS*

1. According to an old legend, **there** is treasure buried on that island.

2. Juan and Pancho just called to let us know **they're** coming for dinner.

3. **There** is a mouse in my closet!

4. I can't wait to see the looks on **their** faces when I tell them the truth.

5. I wonder if **they're** planning to go shopping with us.

6. The children went upstairs to play after clearing **their** plates at dinner.

7. It's **their** decision, so I'll just stay out of it.

8. I don't know what **they're** doing to cause all that noise, but it's giving me a headache!

9. The kids haven't called yet; I'm concerned about **their** being out so late at night.

10. I believe Wynona left her glasses over **there**.

MORE CONFUSING WORDS AND HOMONYMS
QUIZ 1 ANSWERS

1. It was not just a great day; it was **a historic** occasion, and I was feeling **all right**.

2. It takes **a while** to **adapt** to this hot weather when you're from Anchorage.

3. You don't need fancy **stationery** to thank someone—that's **beside** the point.

4. I **cannot** be calm on roller coasters. I ride them with **bated** breath.

5. I have no **flair** for geography: I thought Buffalo was the **capital** of New York, but it's Albany.

6. Where good friends are concerned, my chief **criterion** has always been loyalty.

7. I **prophesied** that if she kept acting that way, she'd get her just **deserts**.

8. You have to be more **discreet** or you'll **virtually** drive your husband up the wall.

9. I've never **wavered** in my enjoyment of Shakespeare's plays, **e.g.**, *Romeo and Juliet*.

10. Let's take the next boat **off** this island. We'll be in **imminent** danger if we wait around.

11. I explained my **principal** reasons for quitting to a **couple of** guys from work.

MORE CONFUSING WORDS AND HOMONYMS
QUIZ 2 ANSWERS

1. Just wait **till** you see one of the most **unusual** buildings in the Midwest.

2. I always buy Acme products because it's a company **that** really cares about the consumer.

3. I was amazed by the **enormousness** of his hands, which held me in a **vise-like** grip.

4. It's not **every day** that I get to spend several hours on my favorite **pastime**.

5. He's one of the **premier** actors of our generation, **regardless** of his messy personal life.

6. It won't **faze** me in the least if you just **set** your drink on the chair next to you.

7. He never **graduated from** high school because he always **flouted** the school rules.

8. He wore a gold **medal** when he **led** the parade yesterday.

9. I think it was a fashion **mistake** to wear such a **minuscule** ring with such a big bracelet.

10. Even here in earthquake country, that **temblor** was a frightening **phenomenon**.

11. I don't have to show up until 10 **o'clock** in the morning. (**OR** 10 **a.m. OR** 10 in the morning)

EFFECTIVE WRITING *QUIZ 1 ANSWERS*

1. While I am in town. Let's visit Golden Gate Park.
   Make a sentence fragment a full sentence: *While I am in town, let's visit Golden Gate Park.*

2. Walking aimlessly down the street, a bus almost clipped me.
   Correct the dangler (the sentence as written says the bus was walking down the street): *As I was walking aimlessly down the street, a bus almost clipped me.* **OR** *Walking aimlessly down the street, I was almost clipped by a bus.*

3. Good employees are prompt, courteous, and they help you when you need it.
   Use parallel construction: *Good employees are prompt, courteous, and helpful.*

4. Several items of evidence were overlooked by police who were investigating the scene of the crime.
   Avoid wordiness: *The police investigators missed evidence left at the crime scene.*

5. It is expected that you will report for work by no later than nine o'clock.
   Use active verbs: *I expect you to report for work by nine o'clock.*

6. There is just one more thing that I want to say before I finish up.
   Avoid wordiness: *I have one more thing to say.*

7. The patient is not unresponsive.
   Be careful with multiple negatives (*not unresponsive*): *The patient is responsive.*

8. Raised in Italy, my grandfather's broken English created problems early on.
   Correct the dangler (the sentence as written says "my grandfather's broken English" was raised in Italy): *My grandfather was raised in Italy, and his broken English created problems early on.* **OR** *Raised in Italy, my grandfather spoke broken English, which created problems early on.*

9. Students will benefit themselves by listening, taking notes, and they should always pay attention.
   Use parallel construction: *Students will benefit themselves by listening, taking notes, and paying attention.*

10. The cars were worn down by the taxi drivers.
    Use active verbs: *The taxi drivers wore down their cars.*

11. After tossing and turning, the alarm came on much too early.
    Correct the dangler (the alarm was not tossing and turning): *After tossing and turning, I was awoken much too early by the alarm.* **OR** *Because I slept restlessly, the alarm woke me much too early.*

12. I have always believed in being thrifty, loyal, and I do high-quality work.
    Use parallel construction: *I have always believed in thrift, loyalty, and high-quality work.*

13. One thing I could say without hesitation is that he is not unreliable.
    Be careful with multiple negatives (*not unreliable*): *One thing I could say without hesitation is that he is reliable.*

EFFECTIVE WRITING *QUIZ 2 ANSWERS*

1. We will utilize the attorneys we have employed to engender the dissolution of our marriage.
   Avoid wordiness: *We have hired attorneys to help us with our divorce.*

2. The boy was hit in the face by the pie as it left the girl's hand.
   Use active verbs to avoid dull writing: *The girl flung the pie, and it exploded in the boy's face.*

3. It was not likely that no one would want to claim ownership of the new sports car.
   Avoid confusing multiple negatives (**not . . . no one**): *Someone will surely want to claim ownership of the new sports car.*

4. We washed the dishes, swept the floor, and the tables were dusted.
   Use parallel construction: *We washed the dishes, swept the floor, and dusted the tables.*

5. While singing in the shower, the bar of soap slipped from her hands.
   Correct the dangler (the soap was not singing): *The bar of soap slipped from her hands as she sang in the shower.*

6. Maria encountered a stranger clad in her parka and blue jeans.
   Descriptive words and phrases should be close to the words they describe: *Maria, clad in her parka and blue jeans, encountered a stranger.*

7. The weather had adverse impacts on our boat, resulting in the necessity of rescuing us from the water.
   Avoid wordiness: *Our boat capsized in the storm, so we needed rescuing.*

8. On a hike with my wife, a bear climbed a tree.
   Correct the dangler (the bear was not hiking with "my wife"): *On a hike with my wife, I saw a bear climb a tree.*

9. Looking back, the dog was following us.
   Correct the dangler (the sentence as written says the dog was looking back): *Looking back, we saw the dog following us.*

10. Jordan did not believe that Serena had embarrassed him unintentionally.
    Avoid pretentious multiple negatives (*not … unintentionally*): *Jordan believed that Serena had embarrassed him intentionally.*

11. Martin could not juggle watching Timmy, making breakfast, and he had a report to write.
    Use parallel construction: *Martin could not juggle watching Timmy, making breakfast, and writing a report.*

12. Like others we questioned, his name was not announced.
    Correct the dangler ("his name" is not what was "like others"): *Like others we questioned, he was not identified by name.*

13. I was wearing the sweater that Amy knitted at the concert.
    Descriptive words and phrases should be close to the words they describe: *At the concert, I was wearing the sweater that Amy knitted.*

14. Lying on a stretcher, they carried him out.
    Correct the dangler ("they" were not lying on a stretcher): *They carried him out lying on a stretcher.*

GRAMMAR MASTERY *TEST ANSWERS*

1. Some of the desserts **were** left by the end of the birthday party.

2. It was **I** and maybe two other people.

3. Dr. Cresta is one of those professors who **do** whatever it takes to get **their** point across.

4. Your brilliant excuses almost **make** up for your tardiness.

5. Neither Jackson nor Jenna is playing hooky. (CORRECT)

6. Neither Jackson nor his family **is** going camping this weekend.

7. Either of us is capable of winning. (CORRECT)

8. All of the class is willing to take part in the prank. (CORRECT)

9. One-third of the eligible population **tends** not to vote in national elections.

10. Not even one-third of the voters **tend** to cast their ballots in national elections.

11. Here **are** the paper clips you requested.

12. She is one of those doctors who make house calls. (CORRECT)

13. **She** and **he** are always fighting.

14. When Toni and **he** come over, we always have a great time.

15. It is we who must decide whether to tax ourselves or cut spending. (CORRECT)

16. Between you and **me**, this class is a joke.

17. **Who** do you think you are to give me advice about dating?

18. Who makes up these English rules anyway? (CORRECT)

19. **Who** do you think should win?

20. **Whom** are you voting for?

21. She is one of the only teachers who **do** what it takes to help **their** students learn joyfully.

22. **Whoever** has the keys gets to be in the driver's seat.

23. We are willing to work with **whomever** you recommend.

24. The thoughts that Ted presented at the meeting were worthwhile. (CORRECT)

25. The thoughts that Ted presented, **which** were about shifting national priorities, were well received.

26. When you do a job so **well**, you can expect a raise.

27. I, **like** most people, try to be considerate of others.

28. Harry smells good. What is the aftershave he is wearing? (CORRECT)

29. Lisa did so well on the test that she was allowed to accelerate to the next level. (CORRECT)

30. Our puppy is the least **hungry** of the litter.

31. He's a man **who** I think defines greatness.

32. Karen should **have** known that her cheap umbrella would break in the storm.

33. Sometimes the effects of our generosity may seem minimal, but our good intentions do make a difference. (CORRECT)

34. Ben thought he had **laid** my jacket on that bench.

35. Our company policy will not allow me to **accept** a gift worth more than $50.

36. They thought we were late, but my wife and I were **already** at the restaurant.

37. **Regardless** of who was there first, we were all very hungry and ready to eat.

38. We could hardly believe the Giants could **lose** the game by that many runs.

39. Isn't it amazing how long that mime can remain completely **stationary**?

40. The department's principal concern is the safety of all employees. (CORRECT)

41. How did they manage to serve cold ice cream in the middle of the vast **desert**?

42. The boss **complimented** Ari on his excellent presentation.

43. The judge did not believe any of **their** stories.

44. Ilana said she wanted to become **an** FBI agent when she grew up.

45. It's not good when **you're** always late like this.

46. To be a good billiards player, you've got to think **further** ahead than just the next shot.

47. I think I'll go **lie** down awhile.

48. The golf course at the resort is lovely, but I prefer **its** swimming pool.

49. Sam and **I** paid the cab fare, and Alejandro paid for dinner.

50. Marta completed five **fewer** problems than I did in the same amount of time.

PUNCTUATION, CAPITALIZATION, AND WRITING NUMBERS *PRETEST ANSWERS*

1. Go **west** three blocks and turn right.

2. He insisted it was based on the **people's** right to know.

3. "How," I asked, "**can** you always be so forgetful?"

4. I want you to meet my best friend, Bill, when he gets here.

5. Although we have a competent staff, bottlenecks do occur.

6. I did not receive the order; therefore, I will not pay my bill. (CORRECT)

7. We offer a variety of drinks, for instance, beer and wine.

8. Is that book **yours**?

9. We have much to do; for example, the carpets need vacuuming.

10. Estimates for the work have been forwarded, and a breakdown of costs has been included. (CORRECT)

11. Because of his embezzling, the company went bankrupt.

12. A proposal that makes harassment of whales illegal has just passed.

13. He is the **president** of our corporation.

14. Paolo hurried to the depot to meet his aunt and two cousins.

15. Finish your job; it is imperative that you do.

16. Sofia and Aidan's house was recently painted. (CORRECT)

17. "Stop it!" I said. "Don't ever do that again."

18. He was born in Ames, Iowa, and still lives there.

19. "Would you like to accompany me?" he asked.

20. I have always had a mental block against **math**.

21. He is a strong, healthy man.

22. To apply for this job, you must have previous experience.

23. Marge, the woman with blond hair, will be our speaker this evening.

24. He thought quickly and then answered the question in complete detail.

25. He asked if he could be excused.

26. It is hailing, not raining.

27. We will grant you immunity if you decide to cooperate with us.

28. You signed the contract; consequently, you must provide us with the raw materials. **OR** You signed the contract. Consequently, you must provide us with the raw materials.

29. I would like, however, to read the fine print first.

30. You are required to bring the following: **sleeping** bag, food, and a sewing kit.

31. The three **companies'** computers were stolen.

32. The **women's** department is upstairs and to your left.

33. It hurt **its** paw.

34. One of the **lawyers** left her briefcase.

35. That's the **Texas** way of doing things.

36. July 5, 1990, was the day I was born.

37. I need to locate four states on the map: Arkansas, Ohio, Illinois, and Utah.

38. The e-mail read, "Hi, Camille. I haven't heard from you in two weeks."

39. The veterinarian said, "Unless **it's** bleeding and doesn't stop, don't worry about it."

40. Not wanting to discuss this with her mother anymore, Wendy declared, "This is her karma, not mine."

41. You must study hard to get good grades at a major university.

42. **One-fourth** of the police force voted for a pay raise.

43. **Thirty-one** people were injured.

44. I owe you **$15**, not $16. **OR** I owe you $15.00, not **$16.00**.

COMMAS AND PERIODS *QUIZ 1 ANSWERS*

1. Ophelia is picking up the food, and I am making the centerpieces.

2. "Yes," Ting said, "I did see the baby panda at the zoo today."

3. Her mother is planning a trip to Portland, Maine, in the fall this year.

4. Patrick's name was on the guest list, wasn't it? (CORRECT)

5. Yes, Mother, I did remember to place the bakery order.

6. Jackson's white cat was born in June 2013 at his farm.

7. Jackson's white cat was born on June 28, 2013, at his farm.

8. You may only bring the bare essentials to the exam, i.e., a watch, a pencil or a pen, paper, and a calculator.

9. Pencils, pens, paper, calculators, etc., will be provided. (CORRECT)

10. I would be hesitant, however, to take the trip alone.

11. He hosted a cowboy-themed party in the big red barn.

12. It looks like A.J. Jefferson Jr. will be our next congressman. **OR** It looks like A.J. Jefferson, Jr., will be our next congressman.

13. If you are interested in working for our company, send us your résumé.

14. My oldest cousin, who lives in Detroit, used to be a policeman.

15. Jonathan Green, M.D., will be the keynote speaker at the conference.

16. The keynote speaker at the conference will be Jonathan Green, M.D.

17. Well, do you think we'll see the sun today?

18. Frank visited the travel agent but still did not book his trip.

19. I want to go now, not later.

20. I really enjoyed the show. **T**he acting was superb. **OR** I really enjoyed the show, **and** the acting was superb.

COMMAS AND PERIODS *QUIZ 2 ANSWERS*

1. I took Angie, the one with the freckles, to the movie last night.

2. Jeremy and I have had our share of arguments.

3. You are, I am sure, telling the truth.

4. She left Albany, New York, on January 18 of that year.

5. I need sugar, butter, and eggs from the grocery store.

6. Dairy products, e.g., milk, butter, eggs, etc., are no longer foods I can eat.

7. Please, Sasha, come home as soon as you can.

8. Although you may be right, I cannot take your word for it.

9. If you decide to cooperate with us, we will grant you immunity.

10. I am typing a letter, and she is talking on the phone.

11. She finished her work and then took a long lunch.

12. Mae said, "Why don't you come up and see me sometime?"

13. You said that I could go, didn't you? (CORRECT)

14. To apply for this job, you must have a Social Security card.

15. He seems to be such a lonely, quiet man, doesn't he?

16. She wore a bright red dress. (CORRECT)

17. She has a good, healthy attitude about her work.

18. On June 7, 2012, Hector earned his computer science degree.

19. I like anchovies on my pizza. **M**y wife hates them. **OR** I like anchovies on my pizza, **but** my wife hates them.

20. Although my wife hates anchovies, I like them on my pizza.

SEMICOLONS AND COLONS *QUIZ 1 ANSWERS*

1. Denise prefers to eat chicken or fish; I'm a vegetarian.

2. The centerpieces had her favorite flowers: roses, carnations, and daisies.

3. They were missing a few things on their camping trip; namely, they forgot sunscreen, towels, and firewood.

4. Please give me some time; I do not want to be rushed.

5. While visiting the beach, we saw pelicans, stingrays, and iguanas.

6. I would like to leave early in the morning; therefore, I am going to bed soon.

7. On our last trip we stayed in Nashville, Tennessee; Atlanta, Georgia; and Orlando, Florida.

8. The girls on the team will have quite a few expenses: uniforms, shoes, equipment, and camp fees.

9. Estella landed her dream summer job: She'll be an intern in a senator's office. (CORRECT **OR** she'll)

10. Roberto can't decide among three careers: dentist, veterinarian, or physical therapist.

11. When Jane leaves, which will be in a few minutes, we can plan her party, but we still better do it quietly. (CORRECT)

12. The players have only one goal: they want to win the Stanley Cup. **OR** The players have only one goal; they want to win the Stanley Cup.

13. I need to buy shampoo, toothpaste, soap, and contact lens solution.

14. Give her a break; she just started working here two days ago!

15. The delegates came from our offices in Region 1, Boston; Region 2, New York; Region 6, Houston; and Region 10, Seattle.

16. Her new supervisor gave her a list of rules to be followed at the office: no making personal phone calls, surfing the Internet, or reading magazines.

17. Jobs were assigned to the shelter volunteers: clean the litter boxes, sweep the floors, feed the cats, and give them water.

18. Max and Sue have been to the Caribbean many times; however, they have not visited St. Lucia.

19. At the camp the children were divided into two groups: those who know how to swim and those who do not.

20. Ashley was late for the rehearsal; she is usually late.

SEMICOLONS AND COLONS *QUIZ 2 ANSWERS*

1. You asked for forgiveness; he granted it to you.

2. We ask, therefore, that you keep this matter confidential.

3. The order was requested six weeks ago; therefore, I expected the shipment to have arrived by now.

4. The American flag has three colors, namely, red, white, and blue. (CORRECT)

5. Clothes are often made from synthetic material, for instance, rayon.

6. If you believe in magic, magical things will happen, but if you don't believe in magic, you'll discover nothing magical. (CORRECT)

7. The orchestra, excluding the violin section, was not up to par.

8. I have been to San Francisco, California; Reno, Nevada; and Seattle, Washington.

9. I need a few items at the store: clothespins, a bottle opener, and napkins.

10. I answered the phone; no one seemed to be on the other end of the line.

11. I wanted a cup of coffee, not a glass of milk. (CORRECT)

12. We have set this restriction: do your homework before watching television.

13. If you can possibly arrange it, please visit us, but if you cannot, let us know.

14. I gave her a lot of money while we were married; therefore, I do not wish to pay her a dime in alimony.

15. We have a variety of desserts, for instance, apple pie, chocolate mousse, and flan.

16. I needed three cards to win the hand, namely, the ten of hearts, jack of diamonds, and king of hearts.

17. I needed three cards to win the hand: the ten of hearts, jack of diamonds, and king of hearts.

18. I would, therefore, like to have an explanation for the missing cash.

19. Nature lovers will appreciate seeing whales, sea lions, and pelicans.

20. He has friends from Iowa and Nebraska, and Illinois is his home state.

QUESTION MARKS AND QUOTATION MARKS
QUIZ 1 ANSWERS

1. "Have you already completed our survey?" the cashier asked.

2. Yan inquired, "Is it supposed to snow tomorrow?"

3. I wonder why Allen left so early this morning.

4. "Are we really planning to drive straight through without stopping?" he asked in amazement.

5. "I hope you don't mind my asking," she said, "but do you realize how tired everyone is going to be by the time we get there?"

6. Shia asked with disbelief, "Are you sure you want to be the one to tell her?"

7. Betty is the one who found out first, isn't she?

8. "Victor asked me what I did yesterday," she said.

9. She said, "T.J. shouted, 'We are not staying at that hotel.'"

10. Carmella wanted to know if you need a ride to the mall. (CORRECT)

QUESTION MARKS AND QUOTATION MARKS
QUIZ 2 ANSWERS

1. He wanted to know when you will be here.

2. "Well," she said, "you certainly didn't waste any time."

3. "Is it almost over?" he asked.

4. "I've had it up to here!" she screamed.

5. The song asks, "Would you like to swing on a star?"

6. Carmen said, "She vowed, 'I'll never leave you.' "

7. "May I have a rain check on that lunch?" I asked.

8. Do you believe the saying, "It is better to vote for what you want and not get it than to vote for what you don't want and get it"?

9. Bernard said, "Waldo asked, 'Who took my pencil sharpener?' "

10. "May I see your ID card?" the clerk asked.

PARENTHESES AND BRACKETS *QUIZ 1 ANSWERS*

1. After standing in line for 30 minutes (or possibly longer), she was able to buy the tickets.

2. My cousin wrote, "I herd [*sic*] a rumor that Jack and Jennifer are getting engaged."

3. I would like to confirm my membership. (The dues check is enclosed.) **OR** I would like to confirm my membership (the dues check is enclosed).

4. Our first meeting will be held at First Central Bank's community room (Main Street branch).

5. We all decided to go out for pizza after the meeting (except for Dan). (CORRECT)

6. I overheard her say, "Our favorite cousin [she meant Dale] will be accompanying us on our trip."

7. Yasir was able to find the book he wanted for a really good price (twenty-five dollars).

8. Luigi moved to this country shortly after he was born (about 1925). (CORRECT)

9. When his family came to the United States, they settled in Washington (state).

10. The first line of his letter said, "My freinds [*sic*], I never thought we would all be together again like this." (CORRECT)

PARENTHESES AND BRACKETS *QUIZ 2 ANSWERS*

1. She requested (actually she pleaded) that her name be withheld.

2. Joe called today (**he**'s been sick) and said he felt better.

3. I can have lunch with you tomorrow (Friday).

4. I hope you are feeling better. (I am sick today.) **OR** I hope you are feeling better (I am sick today).

5. In the movie Vanessa exclaims, "Whatever shall I do if he [the sheriff] comes looking for you tomorrow?"

6. I read in the Mill Valley police log: "Officers were called to disburse [*sic*] attendees at a noisy party."

7. Daniel wanted to know why Mindy felt that way (he really didn't understand it). **OR** Daniel wanted to know why Mindy felt that way. (**He** really didn't understand it.)

8. Mariella told us that when her grandfather was a child, he used to work at a hamburger stand for almost nothing (sixty-five cents an hour**)**.

9. I need to run to the store right away (it's going to close in 20 minutes**)**. **OR** I need to run to the store right away. (**It's** going to close in 20 minutes.)

10. "[**D**]o not go to sleep angry at each other," the author states on page 56.

APOSTROPHES *QUIZ 1 ANSWERS*

1. The movie had **its** desired effect.

2. Both of my **brothers-in-law** live near Durango.

3. Those **girls'** vitality and humor are infectious.

4. ***Women's** Wear Daily* has been called the industry's voice of authority.

5. Those **actresses'** costumes look beautiful on them.

6. Bill and Al had a boat. I was there when **Bill** and Al's boat sank.

7. She always let me stay up past the other **children's** bedtime.

8. In some **people's** opinion, Faulkner is too difficult.

9. I really felt that I got my **money's** worth.

10. Would that **company's** health plan give you peace of mind?

APOSTROPHES *QUIZ 2 ANSWERS*

1. Those old **factories' roofs** have all caved in.

2. The two little **birds' feathers** were ruffled.

3. If it isn't **hers**, then **whose** is it?

4. Joe Wilson said, "I may be biased, but the **Wilsons'** holiday meals are the best."

5. Watch out for the **scissors'** sharp blades. (**OR scissors's**)

6. **We've** been invited to her two **sisters-in-law's** party.

7. **Doesn't** it seem strange that I didn't see that friend of **yours** anywhere?

8. The five injured **sailors'** relatives are waiting outside.

9. Not all **babies'** mothers agree on what constitutes good nutrition.

10. Mr. Simms said none of his fellow **Simmses'** opinions would sway him.

HYPHENS BETWEEN WORDS *QUIZ 1 ANSWERS*

1. The storm blew down a **seventy-foot-tall** tree last night.

2. The tree that blew down last night was seventy feet tall. (CORRECT)

3. My sister is moving from her home next to the **heavily congested** highway.

4. The summer camp was designed for **16-year-old** to **18-year-old** gymnasts.

5. The summer camp was designed for gymnasts 16 years old to 18 years old. (CORRECT)

6. The summer camp was designed for gymnasts 16-18 years old. (CORRECT)

7. Clashes came **one year** after the prime minister took office.

8. It's a **two-hour** meeting, **2:30-4:30** p.m. (Remember: no spaces around hyphens.)

9. If we split the bill evenly, we each owe **thirty-four** dollars.

10. We offer **around-the-clock** coverage.

11. Those **low interest** rates are tempting.

12. He certainly is a slovenly-appearing young man. (CORRECT)

HYPHENS BETWEEN WORDS *QUIZ 2 ANSWERS*

1. She jumped from a **two-story** building.

2. You must **let down** your guard.

3. You certainly have a **go-get-it** nature.

4. The **badly injured** fireman was taken to a hospital.

5. Look **left and right** before you cross the street.

6. The **left-handed** pitcher threw fastballs at almost 100 miles per hour.

7. Do you remember anything you read in the fourth grade? (CORRECT)

8. This is **seventh-grade** reading material.

9. Beware of **high-pressure** telemarketers.

10. That **two-year-old** is adorable.

11. That two-**year-old** child is adorable.

12. That child is two years old. (CORRECT)

HYPHENS WITH PREFIXES AND SUFFIXES *QUIZ 1 ANSWERS*

1. Construction of the **trans-Alaska** oil pipeline had to address issues caused by **permafrost**.

2. Our town's **ex-mayor** has surprised everyone by deciding to run for **reelection**. (**OR re-election**)

3. The safety official **de-emphasized** human error as a factor in the accident.

4. Oh no, I've spilled coffee all over myself and will have to **re-dress** for dinner.

5. Jacob had to sue the manufacturer to obtain full **redress** for his injuries. (CORRECT)

6. According to Aunt Agnes, half of young people today are **semi-illiterate**.

7. Our farming **co-op** includes a rooster and a coop for five chickens.

8. I suppose hiking twelve miles a day for four days is **doable**, but I'd rather not.

9. It is a **truism** that creating a **Cubist-style** painting is easier said than done.

10. Would you have guessed that **ex-Senator** Salazar would become **Governor-elect** Salazar?

HYPHENS WITH PREFIXES AND SUFFIXES *QUIZ 2 ANSWERS*

1. non-Jewish

2. preexisting (**OR** pre-existing)

3. reestablish

4. self-satisfied

5. ex-Marine

6. anti-inflammatory

7. antiwar (**OR** anti-war)

8. error-free

9. self-styled
10. absenteeism

CAPITALIZATION *QUIZ 1 ANSWERS*

1. Don't you love looking at the sky when **Venus** appears next to the **moon**?
2. Leslie said that a highlight of her trip to the **nation's capital** was touring the **White House**.
3. My **grandmother** lives on Fillmore **Street**.
4. I will be excited to listen to our **chief executive officer**, Nancy Williamson, speak today in the auditorium.
5. The new immigration bill has the support of most of our **state's congressional** delegation, including **Senator** Mayhew.
6. I plead not guilty, **Your Honor**.
7. Have you ever visited New England in the **fall**?
8. I told **Uncle** Walter to turn **north** when he reached Broadway, but he got lost because he's not from Madison **County**.
9. Uncle Walter said, "**Please** use left or right, not **north**, **south**, **east**, or **west**."
10. Adriana is dreading **spring quarter** because she has to take **organic chemistry** and Physics 105.
11. Adriana needs to bring the following to her final exam: **two** pencils, scratch paper, a calculator, and a light snack.
12. That was amazing how **coach** Ernie Sasaki led **the** Bulldogs to their first winning season.

CAPITALIZATION *QUIZ 2 ANSWERS*

1. She said, "**Bees** are not the only insects that sting."
2. "You must understand," he pleaded, "**that** I need more time to pay you."
3. Mark Paxton, the **vice president** of the company, embezzled over one million dollars.
4. The **president** of the United States wields much power.
5. I live in the northeastern part of the state, where the climate is colder. (CORRECT)
6. The West, especially California, is famous for its cutting-edge technology. (CORRECT)

7. Have you read *All the King's Men*?

8. I enjoy **summer** more than any other season.

9. Employees of the **company** were laid off with little hope of returning to work.

10. The **Supreme Court** unanimously struck down the proposed **constitutional amendment** today.

11. We saw **director** George Lucas walking down the street.

12. We all stood for the **national anthem** before watching **the** New York Mets play **the** Chicago Cubs.

WRITING NUMBERS *QUIZ 1 ANSWERS*

1. During the first hours after the plane crash, authorities reported **thirty-six** people missing.

2. **Thirty-six** people were reported missing during the first hours after the plane crash.

3. The new stadium will hold **43,520** fans.

4. Bobby grew **0.67** inches in three months. (.67 is less clear.)

5. Next week's lottery jackpot is expected to reach between four million and **five** million dollars. **OR** Next week's lottery jackpot is expected to reach between **4** million and **5** million dollars.

6. Next week's lottery jackpot is expected to reach between $4 million and $5 million. **OR** Next week's lottery jackpot is expected to reach between **4** million dollars and **5** million dollars.

7. The next meeting of the holiday party planning committee will be held on the 31st of October at **noon**.

8. The plane won't arrive until **noon**.

9. Some people now refer to the **forties** and **fifties** as "mid-century." (**OR midcentury**)

10. Some people now refer to the **'40s** and **'50s** as "midcentury." (**OR mid-century**)

WRITING NUMBERS *QUIZ 2 ANSWERS*

1. **One-fifth** of the inventory was ruined in the fire.

2. A **two-thirds** majority is needed to pass the measure.

3. The tree grew only **0.5** inches because of the drought.

4. Her earnings rose from $500 to **$5,000** in one year because of her marketing efforts. **OR** Her earnings rose from **$500.00** to $5,000.00 in one year because of her marketing efforts.

5. I paid her all but the last **seventy-five cents** today. **OR** I paid her all but the last **75 cents** today.

6. We all agreed. **Twenty-five hundred dollars** is a lot of money.

7. **Forty-seven** people were hired last month.

8. Including tax, my new car cost **thirty-two** thousand six hundred seventy-two dollars **and fifty-seven** cents.

9. I will be **twenty-one** years old on December 9.

10. We have only received **0.54** inches of rain this year.

PUNCTUATION, CAPITALIZATION, AND WRITING NUMBERS MASTERY *TEST ANSWERS*

1. I am asking if you would like to roller blade together tomorrow.

2. Yes, Jean, you were right about that answer.

3. He said that the book was "**in** my office if you want to read it," so I took him up on it.

4. Wherever we go, people recognize us.

5. Isabel enjoys the museum although she cannot afford the entrance fee. (CORRECT)

6. His new book is titled *Food **Is My** Favorite Thing*.

7. You are my friend; however, I cannot afford to lend you any more money.

8. Paul Simon sang, "I am a rock; I am an island." (**OR** "I am a rock. I am an island.")

9. I asked Ella, "Did he want his ring back**?**"

10. John F. Kennedy Jr. became a magazine publisher and a pilot before his tragic death. **OR** John F. Kennedy, Jr., became a magazine publisher and a pilot before his tragic death.

11. Your house resembles the **Johnsons'** house.

12. The elections will be held on the first Tuesday of November 2008. (CORRECT)

13. The elections will be held on Tuesday, November 4, 2008, and the polls will be kept open until 8:00 PM.

14. Carl worried about the hurricane but tried to stay calm and help his family. (CORRECT)

15. I favor green and yellow, and purple is her first choice.

16. I need to locate four states on the map, namely, Minnesota, Michigan, California, and Nevada.

17. This is the point that Einstein made: You cannot fix a problem with the problem.

18. Our **philosophy** teacher thinks Einstein meant that we cannot stop war by waging war.

19. Whenever Cheryl is in town, she visits her sister.

20. A **well-reasoned** argument was presented for negotiating a peaceful resolution.

21. The argument for negotiating a peaceful resolution was well reasoned. (CORRECT)

22. A liberally sprinkled dose of humor was very much appreciated. (CORRECT)

23. Our **liberal-minded** clergyman managed to unite the entire congregation.

24. Our clergyman, who united the entire congregation, was **liberal minded**.

25. Jan asked, "What did Joe mean when he said, 'I will see you later'?"

26. I asked the **Wilsons** over for dinner.

27. When I noticed that our dog cut **its** paw, I called the veterinarian right away.

28. "**You're** right to be concerned," said the vet. "I would like to take a look at your dog."

29. Even though **it's** thirty miles to the town where that vet's office is, I wanted to take the drive.

30. The **friendly-looking** vet examined our dog's paw and suggested that we have it bandaged.

31. We had pet insurance but still owed $40 in co-payment fees. (**OR** 40 dollars)

32. Our dog was a semi-invalid until she chewed off the bandage. (CORRECT)

33. I guess she did what any **self-respecting** dog would do by grooming herself.

34. The dog has fully **recovered**, although I will never be the same.

35. Girls in his family wore **hand-me-down** dresses.

36. Wendy thought she knew everything about her mother but found out two years ago that her mother had been married before. (CORRECT)

37. When Wendy asked about this marriage, her mother, Ilse, was hesitant to discuss any details.

38. "She will go to her grave with some secrets," said Wendy.

39. "Do you understand her need for privacy?" Wendy asked her husband.

40. The wealthy became wealthier during the 1990s. (CORRECT)

41. The alarm clock went off at **four** o'clock.

42. Many people dread the **15th** of April in the United States because taxes are due.

43. The check was written for $13,348.15.

44. The check was written for **three hundred** forty-eight dollars and fifteen cents.

INDEX

A

A, an, 61–62
A while, awhile, 67
Abbreviation, acronym, 62
Abbreviations, at end of sentences, 25
Absolutes, 119–120
Academic concerns: course titles vs. academic subjects, 54; degrees, 28, 39
Accept, except, 62
Active voice, 20
Ad, add, 62
Adapt, adopt, 62
Adjectives, 15–17; adverb forms of, 16–17; commas with, before nouns, 26; compound, hyphens with, 41; defined, 15; degrees of, 17; *good, well*, 16–17; phrases used as, 7; proper, 43, 49–52, 55; quizzes, 134–136, 169–171; with sense verbs, 16; *this, that, these, those*, 17
Adjunct, 9
Adverbs, 15–17; defined, 15; degrees of, 17; ending in *-ly*, 16, 41; *good, well*, 16–17; phrases used as, 7; quizzes, 134–136, 169–171; with sense verbs, 16; *very*, 41, 120
Adverse, averse, 62
Advice, advise, 63; quizzes, 139–140, 174–175
Affect, effect, 63; quizzes, 137–138, 172–173
Ages, 42
Aggravate, 63

Ahold, 63
Aid, aide, 63
Ail, ale, 63
Aisle, isle, 63
All-, 43
All ready, already, 63
All right, 63
All together, altogether, 64
Allowed, aloud, 64
All-time record, 64
Allude, elude, refer, 64
Allusion, illusion, 64
Alphabet Juice (Blount), 120
Altar, alter, 64
A.m., p.m., 58, 65
Ambiguous, ambivalent, 64
American Heritage Dictionary, 97, 119
American Usage and Style (Copperud), 120
Amiable, amicable, 65
Amid, amidst, 65
Amount, number, 65
An, a, 61–62
An historic, 65–66
And: independent clauses joined by, 26–27, 31; in numbers, 59; pronouns and nouns linked by, 11–12; subject-verb agreement, 4
And/or, 65
Anecdote, antidote, 65
Anxious, eager, 66
Any more, anymore, 66
Any time, anytime, 66
Apostrophes, 36–40; in contractions, 38; *dos and don'ts*, 37; with initials,

capital letters, and numbers used as nouns, 39; with possessive personal pronouns, 10, 39; with possessive plural nouns, 36–38; with possessive singular nouns, 36, 38, 40; quizzes, 153–154, 188–189; to show joint possession, 38; single quotation marks vs., 39; *till, 'til*, 40, 118; with time or money, 39, 60
Appositive commas, 28
Appraise, apprise, 66
Art movements, 54
As: like vs., 19; pronouns after, 9
As regards, 92
Ascent, assent, 66
Associated Press Stylebook, 51, 55, 57, 67, 118
Assume, presume, 66
Assure, ensure, insure, 66–67
Aural, oral, 67
Averse, adverse, 62
Awhile, a while, 67

B

Backward, backwards, 67
Bacteria, 67
Bail, bale, 67
Baited breath, bated breath, 68
Ball, bawl, 68
Bare, bear, 68
Basically, 68
Beach, beech, 68
Beat, beet, 68
Because since, 68

Bell, belle, 68

Benighted, 68

Bernstein, Theodore M., 78, 97

Berth, birth, 69

Beside, besides, 69

Better, bettor, 69

Biannual, biennial, semiannual, 69

Bite, byte, 69

Bloc, block, 69

Blount, Roy Jr., 120

Boar, boor, bore, 69

Board, bored, 69

Bolder, boulder, 70

Born, borne, 70

Boy, buoy, 70

Brackets, 35; [*sic*], 35, 113; with interruptions, 35; quizzes, 152–153, 187–188; with quotations, 35. *See also* Parentheses

Brake, break, 70

Bremner, John B., 78

Brians, Paul, 76

Bridal, bridle, 70

Bring, take, 70

Broach, brooch, 70–71

Bryson's Dictionary of Troublesome Words, 70, 103

Buoy, boy, 70

Business writing: colons after salutation in business letter, 32; exclamation points in, 48

But, independent clauses joined by, 26–27, 31

Byte, bite, 70

C

Cache, cash, 71

Can, may, 71

Cannon, canon, 71

Cannot, 71

Canvas, canvass, 71

Capital, capitol, 71–72

Capitalization, 49–55; of art movements, 54; to begin sentence after colon, 32; of *city, county*, etc. before proper noun, 54; of course titles vs. academic subjects, 54; of first word of document and after period, 49; of first word of quotation, 54; following question marks, 47; of geographic regions vs. points of compass, 53; of kinship names, 53; of lists following colons, 31–32, 54; of midsentence independent clause or question, 54; *of "the national anthem,"* 54; of nicknames, 53; pretest, 145–147, 181–182; of *the* before proper nouns, 54; of proper nouns, 49–52; quizzes and mastery test, 157–158, 159–160, 191–192, 193–194; of spelled-out decades, 60; of subtitles of works, 55; of titles and offices, 52–53; of titles of works, 54–55

Carat, caret, karat, 72

Careen, career, 72

Careful Writer, The (Bernstein), 78, 97

Cast, caste, 72

Cement, concrete, 72

Censor, censure, 72

Center around, 72–73

Cereal, serial, 73

Chaise lounge, 73

Chicago Manual of Style, 57

Childish, childlike, 73

Chile, chili, 73

Chomping at the bit, 73

Choral, coral, 73

Chorale, corral, 73

Chord, cord, 74

Cite, sight, site, 74

Classic, classical, 74

Clauses: defined, 7; dependent, 7, 13, 28; essential vs. nonessential, 14, 28–29; independent, 7, 26–27, 28, 54; semicolons in sentences with multiple, 31

Cliché, 74

Click, clique, 74

Climactic, climatic, 74

Close proximity, 74

Coarse, course, 74

Cohort, 75

Coin a phrase, 75

Collectable, collectible, 75

Collective nouns, subject-verb agreement, 6

Collide, crash, 75

Colons, 31–32; after salutation in business letter, 32; capitalization of lists following, 31–32, 54; between independent clauses when second explains first, 32; to introduce lists, 31–32; to introduce long quotations, 32; to introduce series of items, 31; quizzes, 149–151, 184–186; semicolons vs., 30, 31

Comma splices, 26

Commas, 25–30; with academic degrees, 28; after dependent clauses starting sentences, 28; after salutation in informal letters, 32; appositive commas, 28; with cities and states, 27; with dates, 27; with *etc.*, 30; with independent clauses, 26–27, 28; with interrupting expressions, 27; with introductory words, 27, 29–30; with *Jr.* and *Sr.*, 27–28; with names directly addressed, 27; with nonessential words, phrases, and clauses, 14, 28–29; in numbers, 58; Oxford commas, 26; with parentheses, 35; quizzes, 147–149, 182–184; with quotations, 29, 33; to separate contrasting parts of sentences, 29; to separate statements from questions, 29; to separate two adjectives before nouns, 26; in series, 25–26, 30–31; with titles used with names, 28; with two adjectives before nouns, 26

Common Errors in English Usage (Brians), 76

Common nouns: capitalizing, in brand names, 51–52; defined, 1; possessives of, ending in *s*, 36

Complement, compliment, 75

Complete, completely, 75

Compound adjectives, 41

Compound nouns: defined, 1; hyphenating, 41; possessives of, 38; subject-verb agreement, 4

Compound verbs, 41

Comprise, 75–76

Concerted, 76

Concrete, cement, 72

Confidant, confident, 76

Connive, conspire, 76

Connote, denote, 76

Consistency: capitalization and punctuation of list items, 31–32; capitalization of titles of works, 54–55; collective noun subject-verb agreement, 6; parallel construction, 21–22; possessives of nouns ending in *s*, 36; singular pronouns, 11; spelling out numbers vs. using figures, 57, 59

Continual, continuous, 77

Contractions, 38

Convince, persuade, 77

Copperud, Roy H., 65, 120

Coral, choral, 73

Cord, chord, 74

Corral, chorale, 73

Council, counsel, 77
Couple (of), 77
Course, coarse, 74
Crash, collide, 75
Craven, 78
Criteria, 78
Currently, 78

D

Daily basis, 78
Dangling modifiers, 22
Dashes, 45; punctuation replaced by, 45; spacing with, 45; subject-verb agreement, 45
Data, 78
Dates: apostrophes in decades, 39, 60; commas with, 27; using figures to express, 59; years beginning sentences, 57
Definite, definitive, 79
Degrees: academic, 28, 39; of adjectives, 17; of adverbs, 17
Denote, connote, 76
Dependent clauses: commas with independent clauses followed by, 28; commas with sentences starting with, 28; defined, 7; with *whoever/whomever*, 13
Desert, dessert, 79
Despise, 79
Device, devise, 79
Dictionary of Modern American Usage, A (Garner), 114
Dictionary of Usage and Style, A (Copperud), 65
Different from, different than, 19, 79
Dilemma, 20–23
Disburse, disperse, 80
Discomfit, discomfort, 80
Discreet, discrete, 80
Disinterested, uninterested, 80
Dock, 80
Dos and don'ts, 37
Drug (dragged), 80
Dual, duel, 80

E

Each, 9
Eager, anxious, 66
Effect, affect, 63; quizzes, 137–138, 172–173
E.g., i.e., 29–30, 81
Either, 9
Either/or, 4
Eke out, 81

Ellipses, 46–47; defined, 46; to express hesitation, changes of mood, etc., 47; with omitted words or sentences, 46; spacing with, 46
Elude, allude, refer, 64
Emigrate, immigrate, 81
Eminent, imminent, 81
Empathy, sympathy, 82
Emulate, imitate, 82
Enormity, 82
Ensure, insure, assure, 66–67
Enthuse, 82
Epitaph, epithet, 82
Epitome, 82
Erstwhile, 83
Essential clauses, 14, 28–29
Etc., et al., 30, 83
Every day, everyday, 83
Ex-, 43
Exacerbate, exaggerate, 83
Except, accept, 62
Exclamation points, 48; in formal business writing, 48; overuse of, 48; replacing periods, 25, 48; to show emotion, emphasis, or surprise, 48

F

Factious, fractious, 83
Faint, feint, 84
Fair, fare, 84
False possessives, 40
Farther, further, 84
Faze, phase, 84
Feat, feet, 84
Fewer, less, 84
Fir, fur, 85
Firstly, 95, 112
Flair, flare, 85
Flammable, inflammable, 85
Flaunt, flout, 85
Flea, flee, 85
Flounder, founder, 85
Flour, flower, 85
Forego, forgo, 86
Foreword, forward, 86
Forth, fourth, 86
Fortuitous, fortunate, 86
Foul, fowl, 86
Fractions: hyphenating, 42, 58; mixed, 59; subject-verb agreement, 5
Fractious, factious, 83
Free gift, 86
Fulsome, 86
Fun, 87

Fur, fir, 85
Further, farther, 84

G

Gait, gate, 87
Gamut, 87
Gantlet, gauntlet, 87
Garner, Bryan A., 114
Gel, jell, 87
Gilt, guilt, 87
Glib, 88
Good, well, 16–17
Graduate, 88
Graffiti, 88
Grammar: mastery test, 144–145, 179–181; pretest, 125–127, 161–163
Grill, grille, 88
Grisly, gristly, grizzly, 88
Guerrilla, 88
Guilt, gilt, 87

H

Hair, hare, 88
Hall, haul, 88
Halve, have, 89
Hangar, hanger, 89
Hanged, hung, 89
Have, of used in place of, 19
Heal, heel, 89
Healthful, healthy, 89
Hear, here, 89
Helping verbs, 2
Here, 5
Heroin, heroine, 89
Historic, an, 65–66
Hoard, horde, 89
Hoarse, horse, 90
Hole, whole, 90
Holy, wholly, 90
Homage, 90
Hone in, 90
Hot water heater, 90
Hung, hanged, 89
Hyphens, 40–45; with ages, 42; to avoid confusion, 44; for clarification, 42; common misunderstandings about, 40; with compound adjectives, verbs, or nouns, 41; with double last names, 43; looking up use of, 43, 45; overuse of, 43; with prefixes and suffixes, 43–45, 156, 190–191; quizzes, 154–156, 189–191; with *re-*, 44; replacing slashes, 114; with

Hyphens (continued)
  self-, ex-, all-, 43; spacing around, 40, 42; with spelled-out numbers, 42, 58; with very and -ly adverbs, 41; between words, 41–43, 154–155, 189–190

I

Idle, idol, idyll, 90
I.e., e.g., 29–30, 81
Illusion, allusion, 64
Imitate, emulate, 82
Immigrate, emigrate, 81
Imminent, eminent, 81
Impact, 91
Imply, infer, 91
In, into, 20
In order to, 92
In regard(s) to, with regard(s) to, 92
Incite, insight, 91
Include, 91–92
Incomparables, 119–120
Incredible, incredulous, 92
Independent clauses: capitalization of midsentence, 54; commas with, 26–27, 28; defined, 7; semicolons between, 31. See also Sentences
Indirect questions, 47
Infinitives, 3
Inflammable, flammable, 85
Ingenious, ingenuous, 92
Initials, plurals of, 39
Insure, assure, ensure, 66–67
Interrupting expressions: brackets for, 35; commas with, 27; dashes with, 45; subject-verb agreement, 4–5
Introductory words: commas with, 27, 29–30; semicolons before, 30
Irony, 93
Irregardless, 93
Irregular nouns, 37
Is is, 93
Isle, aisle, 63
It is, it was, 21
Italics: for sic, 35; for titles of works, 33
It's, its, 10, 93

J

Jell, gel, 87
Jibe, jive, 93–94
Jr., 27–28
Just, 94
Just deserts, 79

K

Karat, carat, caret, 72
Kindergartner, 94
Knew, new, 94
Kudos, 94

L

Language, concrete vs. vague, 20
Lastly, 95
Latter, 95
Laxadaisical, 95
Lay, lie, 95–96; quizzes, 138–139, 173–174
Lead, led, 96
Leak, leek, 96
Less, fewer, 84
Lessen, lesson, 96
Let he who is without sin. . ., 97
Liable, libel, likely, 97
Lie, lay, 95–96; quizzes, 138–139, 173–174
Lightening, lightning, 97
Like, 18, 19, 97
Likely, 97
Linking verbs, 2
Lists: capitalization and ending punctuation, 31–32, 54; colons before, 31, 54; etc. vs. et al. with, 83. See also Series
Literally, 98
Loan, lone, 98
Loath, loathe, 98
Loose, lose, 98

M

Mail, male, 98
Maize, maze, 99
Manner, manor, 99
Marquee, marquis, 99
Marry, merry, 99
Marshal, martial, 99
Masterful, masterly, 99
Material, materiel, 99
May, can, 71
Medal, meddle, metal, mettle, 99–100
Media, 100
Meretricious, 100
Merriam-Webster's Dictionary of English Usage, 5
Mic, 100
Miner, minor, 100
Minuscule, 101
Misnomer, 101
Modern American Usage, 80, 84
Modifiers: dangling, 22; misplaced, 23
Moral, morale, 101

More importantly, most importantly, 101
Morning, mourning, 101
Muscle, mussel, 101

N

Namely, 29, 30
Names of people: capitalization of kinship names, 53; commas with degrees or titles, 28; commas with, directly addressed, 27; commas with Jr. or Sr., 27–28; hyphens with double last names, 43; nicknames, 53; plurals of, 38; possessives of, 36, 37, 38
Names of places: capitalization of city, county, etc. before, 54; capitalization of geographic regions, 53; commas with cities and states, 27
Naval, navel, 101
Negatives, double, 21
Neither, 9
Neither/nor, 4
Neither. . .or, 102
New, knew, 94
New record, 64
None, 5
Nonessential clauses, 14, 28–29
Nonplussed, 102
Not just, 94
Notoriety, 102
Nouns: collective, subject-verb agreement with, 6; common, 1, 36, 51–52; compound, 1, 4, 38, 41; defined, 1; linked with pronouns by and or or, 11–12; phrases used as, 7; plurals of initials, capital letters, and numbers used as, 39; possessives of, 36–38, 40; quizzes on finding, 127–128, 163–164; regular vs. irregular, 36–37. See also Proper nouns; Subjects
Number, amount, 65
Numbers. See Writing numbers

O

Object of the preposition, 18
Object pronouns, 8–9, 12
Of: subject-verb agreement and phrases beginning with, 4; used in place of have, 19
Off of, 103
Oneself, 10
Or: independent clauses joined by, 26–27, 31; pronouns and nouns

linked by, 12; subject-verb agreement, 4
Oral, aural, 67
Ordinance, ordnance, 103
Orwell, George, 120
Overdo, overdue, 103
Overly, 103
Oxford commas, 26

P

Pail, pale, 103
Pain, pane, 103
Palate, palette, pallet, 104
Parallel construction, 21–22
Parentheses, 34–35; for clarifications and asides, 34; comma placement with, 35; punctuation of complete sentences in, 34; quizzes, 152–153, 187–188; subject-verb agreement, 35. *See also* Brackets
Parish, perish, 104
Parody, satire, 104
Participles, 22
Particles, initial negative, 93
Passed, past, 104
Passive voice, 20
Past history, 104
Pastime, past time, 104
Peace, piece, 104
Peak, peek, pique, 104
Peal, peel, 105
Pedal, peddle, 105
Peer, pier, 105
Penultimate, 105
Percent, 5, 105
Periods: with abbreviations at end of sentences, 25; after indirect questions, 47; capitalization after, 49; with complete sentences in parentheses, 34; at end of sentences, 25; with *et al.* and *etc.*, 83; exclamation points replacing, 25, 48; question marks replacing, 25, 47; quizzes, 147–149, 182–184; with quotation marks, 33; semicolons replacing, 30
Perpetrate, perpetuate, 105
Persecute, prosecute, 105
Persuade, convince, 77
Phase, faze, 84
Phenomenon, 105–106
Phrasal verbs, 2
Phrases: beginning with *of*, subject-verb agreement with, 4; defined, 7; essential vs. nonessential, 28–29

Piece, peace, 104
Pique, peak, peek, 104
Pistil, pistol, 106
Place names. *See* Names of places
Plain, plane, 106
Plum, plumb, 106
P.m., a.m., 58, 65
Point in time, 106
Pole, poll, 106
Poor, pore, pour, 106–107
Possessive pronouns, 10
Possessives: amounts of time or money as, 39; of compound nouns, 38; false possessives, 40; with joint ownership, 38; of nouns, 36–38, 40; of personal pronouns, 10, 39; of words ending in *s*, 36, 37, 40; of words ending in *y*, 40
Pray, prey, 107
Precipitate, precipitous, 107
Predominately, 107
Prefixes, 43–44; confusing without hyphens, 44; defined, 43; ending in same vowel that begins root word, 43; hyphens with, 43–44; before proper nouns or adjectives, 43; quizzes on hyphens with, 156, 190–191; *re-*, 44; *self-, ex-, all-*, 43
Premier, premiere, 107
Prepositions, 18–20; *in, into*, 20; defined, 18; *different from, different than*, 19, 79; *of* vs. *have*, 19; *as, as if, as though, the way*, 19; *like*, 18, 19; phrases used as, 7; quizzes, 136–137, 171–172; sentences ending with, 18
Presently, 107
Presume, assume, 66
Principal, principle, 107
Profit, prophet, 108
Prone, supine, 108
Pronouns, 7–12; caution on apostrophes with, 10, 39; consistency with singular pronouns, 11; defined, 7–8; following *than* or *as*, 9; linked with nouns by *and* or *or*, 11–12; object pronouns, 8–9, 12; possessive pronouns, 10; quizzes, 130–131, 165–167; reflexive pronouns, 10–11; subject pronouns, 8, 9, 12; *this, that, these, those*, 17; *who, which, that*, 9, 14–15, 122
Proper adjectives: capitalizing, 49–52, 55; prefixes before, 43

Proper nouns: capitalization of, 49–52; capitalization of *city, county*, etc. before, 54; capitalization of *the* before, 54; defined, 1; possessives of, 36, 37, 38; prefixes before, 43. *See also* Names of people; Names of places
Prophecy, prophesize, prophesy, 108
Prosecute, persecute, 105
Proximity, close, 74
Punctuation: mastery test, 159–160, 193–194; pretest, 145–147, 181–182
Purposely, purposefully, 108

Q

Question marks, 47–48; after direct questions, 47; capitalization following, 47; with half statement/half question, 48; not used with indirect or rhetorical questions, 47; quizzes, 151–152, 186–187; with quotation marks, 48; replacing periods, 25, 47
Questions: capitalization of midsentence, 54; commas to separate statements from, 29; indirect, 47; rhetorical, 47
Quotation, quote, 108
Quotation marks, 33–34; double, 33; with nonstandard expressions, 33; with periods and commas, 33; with question marks, 48; quizzes, 151–152, 186–187; with quotations longer than one paragraph, 34; single, 33–34, 39; spacing between single and double, 33; for titles of works, 33
Quotations: brackets with, 35; capitalization of first word of, 54; colons to introduce, 32; commas with, 29; within quotations, 33

R

Rack, wrack, 109
Raise, raze, 109
Rap, wrap, 109
Re-, 44
Real, reel, 109
Reason being is, 109
Reason is because, 109
Reek, wreak, 109
Refer, allude, elude, 64
Reflexive pronouns, 10–11

Regular nouns, 36–37
Reign, rein, 110
Relish in, 110
Renown, 110
Rest, as they say, is history, 110
Rest, wrest, 110
Restaurateur, 110
Retch, wretch, 110
Reticent, 110
Reverend, 111
Review, revue, 111
Rhetorical questions, 47
Riff, rift, 111
Right, rite, write, 111
Ring, wring, 111
Road, rode, rowed, 111
Role, roll, 111
Root words, 43
Run-on sentences, 26
Rye, wry, 111

S

Satire, parody, 104
Saver, savor, 112
Scent, sent, 112
Secondly, thirdly, fourthly, 112
Self-, 43
Semiannual, biannual, biennial, 69
Semicolons, 30–31; colons vs., 30, 31; before introductory words, 30; quizzes, 149–151, 184–186; between sentences, 30; in sentences with multiple clauses, 31; in series containing commas, 30–31
Sensual, sensuous, 112
Sentence fragments, 23
Sentences: beginning with numbers, 57; capitalization of independent clause or question in middle of, 54; colons between, when second explains first, 32; commas to separate contrasting parts of, 29; ending with prepositions, 18; parallel construction, 21–22; in parentheses, 34; periods at end of, 25; run-on, 26; semicolons between, 30; word order in, 22–23. *See also* Independent clauses
Serf, surf, 112
Serial, cereal, 73
Series: colon to introduce, 31–32; commas in, 25–26, 30–31; semicolons in, 30–31. *See also* Lists
Set, sit, 112
Sew, so, sow, 113

Shear, sheer, 113
[*sic*], 35, 113
Sight, site, cite, 74
Simplistic, 113
Since, because, 68
Site, sight, cite, 74
Slash (/), 113–114
Sleight, slight, 114
Snuck, 114
So, sew, sow, 113
Soar, sore, 114
Sole, soul, 114
Some, sum, 114
Son, sun, 114
Spacing: with AM or PM, 58; around hyphens, 40, 42; with dashes, 45; with ellipses, 46; between single and double quotation marks, 33
Split infinitives, 3
Sr., 27–28
Staid, stayed, 115
Stair, stare, 115
Stake, steak, 115
Stationary, stationery, 115
Steal, steel, 115
Step, steppe, 115
Stomping grounds, 115
Straight, strait, 115
Strategy, stratagem, 116
Subject pronouns, 8, 9, 12
Subjects: defined, 2; how to find, 2–3; quizzes on finding, 127–128, 163–164; underlining, 1
Subject-verb agreement, 3–7; with *and*, 4; with collective nouns, 6; with dashes, 45; with distances, period of time, sums of money, etc., 6; with *here* and *there*, 5; with interrupting expressions, 4–5; with *none*, 5; with *or, either/or, neither/nor*, 4; with parentheses, 35; with phrases beginning with *of*, 4; with portions, 5; with pronouns, 8, 9; quizzes, 128–130, 164–165; singular vs. plural verbs, 3; subjunctive mood, 6–7; with *who, that, which*, 9
Subjunctive mood: defined, 6; subject-verb agreement, 6–7
Subtitles, 55
Suffixes, 44–45; beginning with same letter that ends root word, 44; defined, 44; not usually hyphenated, 44; quizzes on hyphens with, 156, 190–191;

using discretion with hyphenating, 45
Sum, some, 114
Sun, son, 114
Sundae, Sunday, 116
Supine, prone, 108
Suppose to, 116
Surf, serf, 112
Sympathy, empathy, 82

T

Tack, tact, 116–117
Tail, tale, 117
Take, bring, 70
Taught, taut, 117
Team, teem, 117
Temblor, 117
Tenant, tenet, 117
Than, pronouns after, 9
Than, then, 117
That, who, which, 9, 14–15, 122; quizzes, 133–134, 168–169
That is, 29–30
The, capitalization before proper nouns, 54
The national anthem, 54
Their, there, they're, 117–118; quizzes, 140–141, 175–176
There is, there are, 5, 21
There's, 5
They and *their*, with singular pronouns, 11
This, that, these, those, 17
Those kind of, 118
Till, 'til, 40, 118
Titles and offices: capitalization of, 52–53; commas with, 28
Titles of courses, 54
Titles of works: capitalization of, 54–55; quotation marks or italics for, 33
To, too, two, 118
Tort, torte, 118
Tortuous, torturous, 118
Totally, 118
Toward, towards, 118
Transpire, 118
Tremblor, 119
Troop, troupe, 119
Truly, 119
Turbid, turgid, 119

U

Uninterested, disinterested, 80
Unique, 119–120
Utilize, 120

V

Vain, vane, vein, 120
Venal, venial, 120
Verbs: compound, 41; defined, 1–2;
 how to find, 2–3; infinitives, 3;
 quizzes on finding, 127–128,
 163–164; types of, 2; underlining,
 1. *See also* Subject-verb
 agreement
Verses, versus, 120
Very, 41, 120
Viable, 120
Vial, vile, 121
Vice, vise, 121
Virgule, 113–114
Virtually, 98
Voice, active vs. passive, 20

W

Waist, waste, 121
Wait, weight, 121
Waiver, waver, 121
Warn, worn, 121
Warrantee, warranty, 121
Wary, weary, 121
Way, weigh, 122
Ways to go, 122
Weak, week, 122
Weather, whether, 122

Webster's New World College Dictionary,
 108
Well, good, 16–17
Whether or not, 122
Which, who, that, 9, 14–15, 122;
 quizzes, 133–134, 168–169
While, wile, 122
Who, subject-verb agreement, 8, 9
Who, which, that, 9, 14–15, 122;
 quizzes, 133–134, 168–169
Who, whom, 12, 13; quizzes, 131–134,
 167–169
Whoever, whomever, 13–14; quizzes,
 131–133, 167–168
Whole, hole, 90
Wholly, holy, 90
Who's, whose, 10, 123
With regard(s) to, in regard(s) to, 92
Won't, wont, 123
Words on Words (Bremner), 78
Worn, warn, 121
Wrack, rack, 109
Wrap, rap, 109
Wreak (wreck) havoc, 123
Wreak, reek, 109
Wrest, rest, 110
Wretch, retch, 110
Wring, ring, 111
Write, right, rite, 111

Writing, effective, 20–23; active vs.
 passive voice, 20; concrete vs.
 vague language, 20; dangling
 modifiers, 22; double negatives,
 21; misplaced modifiers, 22;
 overuse of *there is/are, it is/was*, etc.,
 21; parallel construction, 21–22;
 quizzes, 142–144, 177–179;
 sentence fragments, 23. *See also*
 Business writing
Writing numbers, 57–60; beginning
 sentences, 57; commas in, 58;
 dates, 59; decades, 39, 60;
 decimals, 59; fractions, 42, 58, 59;
 hyphens with ages, 42; hyphens
 with spelled-out numbers, 42, 58;
 large numbers, 59; money, 58, 59;
 quizzes, pretest, and mastery test,
 145–147, 158–160, 181–182,
 192–194; time of day, 58–59;
 using figures vs. spelling out
 numbers, 57; when to use *and*
 in spelled-out numbers, 59;
 years, 57
Wry, rye, 111

Y

Yoke, yolk, 124
You're, your, 124

GrammarBook.com is your site for helpful rules, real-world examples, and fun quizzes.

Free Online English Usage Rules

Grammar, Punctuation, and Other English Rule Info

✓ Finding Subjects and Verbs

✓ Subject and Verb Agreement

✓ Commas and Semicolons

✓ Vocabulary, Spelling, and Commonly Confused Words

Quizzes on Each Topic Covered in the Book

✓ Get scored instantly.

✓ Explanations for each quiz question.

✓ Take interactively or download and reproduce the quizzes.

Premium Subscription Levels!

For Instructors & Employers

✓ Unlimited number of student/employee logins.

✓ Quiz results tallied and organized in account automatically.

✓ Makes grading quizzes and explaining answers a thing of the past.

For Grammar Enthusiasts

✓ One subscription works for an entire family, classroom, or office.

✓ Take the quizzes online or download and copy them.